RUGBY FITNESS TRAINING

TRAINING

A Twelve-Month Conditioning Programme

RUGBY FITNESS TRAINING

A Twelve-Month Conditioning Programme

Ben Wilson CSCS

THE CROWOOD PRESS

First published in 2006 by
The Crowood Press Ltd
Ramsbury, Marlborough
Wiltshire SN8 2HR

www.crowood.com

This impression 2012

British Library Cataloguing-in-Publication Data
A catalogue record for this book is available from the British Library.

ISBN 978 1 86126 850 1

Photography by Andy Mills, Saul Wilson and Monika Wilson.

Disclaimer
Please note that the author and the publisher of this book do not
accept any responsibility whatsoever for any error or omission, nor
any loss, injury, damage, adverse outcome or liability suffered as a
result of the use of any of the information contained in this book, or
reliance upon it. Since conditioning exercises can be dangerous and
could involve physical activities that are too strenuous for some
individuals to engage in safely, it is essential that a doctor be
consulted before undertaking training.

Typeset by Florence Production Ltd, Stoodleigh, Devon
Printed and bound in Spain by Graphycems.

Contents

For my dearest mother, and in loving memory of James Durkin.

Acknowledgements

There are many people whom I would like to thank for helping me write this book. I would like to thank The Crowood Press for producing this work. A huge thanks must be said to Aubrey Wilson who, as well as being my grandfather, was my adviser, editor, reference source and everything else throughout this process. I would also like to acknowledge the support of my family – Clive, Jo, Vanessa and Charles – and special mention to my brother Saul and his wife Monika for their help.

A huge thank-you goes to all the other people who made this happen: Pippa Durrant for starting the process, Andrew Mills for the photographs, Paul and Simon for putting up with me writing this while travelling, Michelle Thomas for her advice on side-stepping, Ollie Martin of Take Shape (www.t-shape.co.uk) for the use of his facilities, and everyone else who has offered me encouragement and support throughout this process.

Preface

Rugby Union is a global sport, played in over a hundred countries throughout the world.[1] Since the advent of professionalism in 1995 the game's popularity has been on the rise. Playing numbers have increased both in established rugby countries and in some emerging nations.

Rugby is a demanding sport, requiring the players to engage in physical contact for eighty minutes while constantly making decisions and ensuring they are in the right place at the right time to make a play. The conditioning levels of the professional players are now at the highest the sport has ever seen. These new levels have been attained as a consequence of the athletes being able to train full time using the latest scientific-based training techniques as devised by their strength and conditioning coach.

To break into the semi- or full-time professional ranks, aspiring players know they must be in good physical condition. This has led to an increased focus on personal fitness throughout the amateur level. However, the increased awareness of wanting to improve conditioning has not been accompanied by an increased knowledge of how to do it.

As a player, your goal may be to get into the club's first team, to improve your level of play, or maybe win a full-time contract within the professional ranks. But whatever your goals may be, it is essential that you use a successful rugby-specific fitness programme.

To gain optimal results from your training programme it needs to use the right exercises, in the right proportions, at the appropriate time of the year. To know what is right for you and your sport, the principles of periodization are applied to the design of your conditioning routine.

Periodization is the theory that underlies the training programmes followed by every professional sportsman in the world. The concept covers all aspects of a training routine, and allows athletes to achieve consistently better levels of fitness and performance year after year. But in spite of its unquestionable success and common place amongst the élite, the theory has failed to spread to the amateur sportsman found in gymnasiums and sports clubs across the country.

This book is the first on Rugby Union to teach the underlying theory of conditioning programmes, and bridges the gap between the in-depth texts on periodization[2,3] and the reader. It can be read by players from young to old who are looking to improve their performance on the rugby field. On completing the book not only will you understand why a programme is designed as it is, but you will also know how to design and use your very own. After you have read the text and followed the ten steps to design your personal training programme, the book will become a reference to refer back to during your training routine and refresh your knowledge on correct exercise techniques.

The first chapter explains the basics of the human body, physical training and Rugby Union, and gives the reader a greater understanding of the exercise principles, the theory, and the demands that Rugby Union imposes on the body.

The second chapter introduces the training methods used to improve your physical attributes, and the basic routines used within each method. This will provide the reader with a clear picture of how to train for the sport.

The following two chapters contain all the exercises in the training methods, and the tests used to monitor the physical attributes. These chapters will act as a reference on how to accomplish everything performed during the programme.

Chapter 5 introduces periodization, the art of structuring conditioning programmes. The basic principles are explained, together with the general application of this theory to training.

Chapter 6 discusses how to design a fitness programme specifically for Rugby Union.

The routines used within each method are clarified, along with when to perform the training, and how it is to be varied.

Chapter 7 shows how to design your personal conditioning programme step by step. The ten steps take you through the process of creating your very own twelve-month fitness regime.

The final chapter gives a year-long example of how the conditioning programme can be designed and implemented into your life. This should clarify and cement all the principles learnt in previous chapters.

The Appendix contains the blank forms and tables needed to design your own twelve-month conditioning programme.

The book gives the reader the conditioning programme and knowledge to fulfil their true playing potential. I wish you the best of luck, and success in your future rugby performances.

CHAPTER 1

Fitness Fundamentals

This chapter examines the mechanics of the human body, how physical abilities can be classified, and which of these characteristics are necessary to succeed on the rugby pitch. The chapter then explains the theory and relevant issues associated with training and improved performance.

You may be tempted to turn straight to the training section of the book, but this would be a mistake. Understanding the fundamentals of the human body, your own physical abilities, and training theory will ensure maximum benefit from the training programme. The great Michael Schumacher puts much of his success down to his knowledge and understanding of the internal combustion engine, the physics of speed and the way to get the best from himself. In the same way, by learning how the body works – why and what you are training for – higher levels of performance will be attained.

THE FUNDAMENTALS OF THE HUMAN BODY

The following section looks at the musculoskeletal system, the mechanics of muscles, and how the body powers the muscles.

The Musculoskeletal System

The human body is comprised of various tissues, organs and structures. The primary concern with regard to sporting performance is the musculoskeletal system, which is comprised of bones, connective tissues and muscles.

Bones

There are over 200 bones in the human body, and their primary purpose is to provide a framework for the body and so protect the organs. Bones come in a variety of shapes and sizes, being made up from hard (compact) or soft (cortical) bone, or a mixture of both. The contribution of bones to sporting performance and everyday life usually goes unnoticed except when injury occurs from the bone being subjected to excessive forces; this can result in a fracture.

Joints

A joint is where two or more bone ends meet. There are different types of joint that allow varying degrees of movement in one or more directions. Joints may allow very limited movement – for example, the joints of the bones in the skull – to a large range of movement – for example, the shoulder joint. The movement of the joints governs the mechanics on how the body moves, and in what ways.

Ligaments

Ligaments are attached from bone to bone across a joint, and are designed to prevent unwanted movement. Ligaments do not participate in normal movements, but come into effect if the joint is forced in an unwanted direction when they hold the bones together and prevent further movement in this wrong direction. When a force greater than the ligaments' strength is applied to a joint, they are either partially or fully torn. A torn ligament can no longer protect the joint from excessive movements. To repair a ligament that has been completely torn, surgery is usually required.

Cartilage

There are different types of cartilage. Sporting movements rely on cartilage found in the joints, the most common of which is articular cartilage lining the bone ends. Articular cartilage becomes lubricated during movement, thus allowing the bone ends to move freely past each other without undue friction. Cartilage serves to absorb the forces that are transmitted through the bones.

Tendons

A tendon is the end of a muscle which is attached to the bone. The function of tendons is to join the muscle into the bone and transmit the forces from the muscle to produce movement. The tendons are often attached to the bone at the joint, although they can be attached anywhere along the bones. The area where the muscle becomes a tendon is often a source of injury, as it is the most common place for slight tendon tears to occur.

Muscles

In sport the main area of interest is with the muscles. There are hundreds of muscles in the human body. Fitness training mostly focuses upon the prime movers – the larger muscles that create movement. These are the ones you can see when you look in the mirror. The importance of these to performance is demonstrated by the fact that nearly all professional athletes these days have a rippling physique surrounding their frame.

Structure of a muscle: A muscle is made up from many thousands of muscle fibres; at the smallest level a muscle fibre is comprised of two types of molecular chains (combinations of different molecules). Millions of these chains slide past each other to cause the muscle to change length. The thousands of muscle fibres are grouped together into bundles of fibres, and this process is repeated until the bundles are grouped together into the muscles seen on our body. The end of the muscle becomes a tendon where it is joined on to the bone.

Muscle fibres: The thousands of muscle fibres found within a muscle can be classified under two main categories: fast- and slow-twitch fibres:

Slow-twitch fibres produce less forceful and slower contractions than fast-twitch fibres, but are able to produce many contractions without fatigue. Slow-twitch fibres are used for movements that do not require large amounts of force to be produced, such as walking, or lightly jogging to the next scrum.

Fast-twitch fibres produce forceful, powerful contractions but are more susceptible to fatigue. Fast-twitch fibres would be used when large forces are required, for instance pushing in a scrum, or sprinting to score a try.

The body recruits a mixture of fast-twitch and/or slow-twitch fibres, depending upon the requirement of the exercise. To perform a 30m sprint the body recruits the fast-twitch fibres, when performing a light jog it will recruit slow-twitch fibres, while an 800m run will use a variety of both fibres to perform the activity.

The muscles in the body have different proportions of slow-twitch and fast-twitch fibres. How the fibres are distributed is largely genetic, but can be slightly altered by training techniques.

Muscle mechanics: A muscle contraction occurs when the tiny molecular chains slide past each other. The simultaneous movement of these many millions of chains within a muscle creates the muscle contraction seen to the naked eye. The muscle pulls on the bone it is attached to, through its tendon, thereby creating movement of the limbs.

A muscle contraction can be classified in three ways, depending on the how the muscle changes length.

Concentric contraction: The muscle shortens during the contraction – for example, if you kick a ball, the quadriceps (thigh) muscle shortens as your leg straightens.

Eccentric contraction: The muscle lengthens while contracting – for example, when you lower a weight slowly back downwards, or when slowing down a body part, the muscle undergoes an eccentric contraction. This means that although it is getting longer, it is still contracting – indeed, if it were not, the weight would fall quickly to the floor, or the body part would stop moving only when the joint locked straight at the end of its movement range.

Isometric contraction: The muscle does not change length during the contraction: for example, when equally pushing against another player in a ruck, scrum or maul, the muscles are still working but there has been no movement or change in length of the actual muscle.

Muscles and movement: A muscle produces movement of the body by pulling against the bone to which it is attached. To facilitate movement, the muscles around the joint must be co-ordinated so that some muscles are contracting while others are relaxing, and some are stabilizing the joints. Through the co-operation of these muscles, movement can occur. Each muscle involved in a movement can be classified, dependent upon the role it plays.

Agonists: The muscle(s) that contract during the movement. The muscle(s) can contract isometrically, concentrically and/or eccentrically.

Antagonist: The muscle(s) that oppose the agonist muscle(s); the antagonists must relax to allow movement to occur.

Stabilizers: The muscle(s) that stabilize the joint. These muscle(s) contract around the joint, holding it in place so that the agonists can pull against the bone to produce the required movement.

If you analyse what happens when you kick a ball, the above labels in the diagram can be applied to the muscle groups involved. When striking the ball, the quadriceps muscles are working as the agonist, contracting

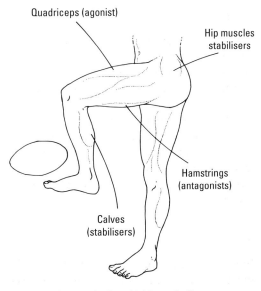

The muscles used when kicking a ball.

concentrically to bring the foot upwards and kick the ball. The hamstrings are the antagonist muscle, and must relax to allow the movement to occur. The calves, shin muscles and the muscles of the hip are the stabilizers, holding the thigh and foot in place to allow the movement to occur correctly, with maximum force.

It is through these methods that all movement occurs, and the greater the body's ability to contract the agonist and relax antagonist, the more efficient and forceful the movement can be.

Neuromuscular Co-Ordination

The ability to co-ordinate the muscles and the actions they perform is referred to as 'neuromuscular co-ordination'. The messages from the brain are sent through the nerves into the muscles telling them how to act. The network of nerves is referred to as the central nervous system (CNS). The messages passed through the central nervous system tell the muscles whether to act as an agonist, antagonist or stabilizer, and how forcefully they need to contract. It is through these signals to the appropriate muscles that all movement is produced.

The greater the number of times the body is required to perform a movement, the more efficient it becomes at sending messages to co-ordinate the muscles involved. This is the origin of the saying 'practice makes perfect'. Through repeating a task over and over again, improved neuromuscular co-ordination allows for less energy to be expended for that given task, and for the achievement of higher forces, speeds and accuracy. The regime of kicking practice followed by Johnny Wilkinson serves as an example of this.

Motor units: A motor unit is the name given to the signal from the brain and the muscle

fibres it stimulates to contract. The body has many motor units within a muscle, which stimulate varying amounts of fast- and slow-twitch muscle fibres. Some motor units result in many fibres being contracted to produce large amounts of force, while others produce very low amounts of force by recruiting only a small number of fibres.

The larger motor units – those that produce greater amounts of force – cannot always be recruited as and when required, but can be invoked under certain circumstances. This can be seen from examples of a mother lifting a car off their child. In these extraordinary circumstances the people involved are able to recruit their largest motor units to move this normally fixed object. Through training, the athlete is able to use regularly the larger motor units, allowing higher levels of strength and performance to be achieved.

Powering the Muscles

As stated previously, movement occurs through the contracting muscles pulling on the bones to which they are attached. The movement produced is from the microscopic molecular chains sliding past each other, and in order to do this, energy is needed to overcome the frictional forces between the chains: it comes from one type of molecule.

The energy currency: The energy for a muscle contraction comes from breaking the

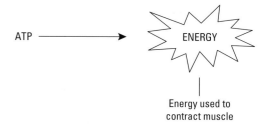

Overview of how energy is produced from ATP.[4]

chemical bonds in a molecule called ATP (adenosine tri-phosphate). The energy produced is used to make the chains of molecule within a muscle fibre slide past each other and therefore make the muscle contract.

The ATP molecule is broken down into energy and an ADP molecule. The body reconverts the ADP back into ATP to repeat the process. There are only limited stores of ATP, therefore the body must continually produce this molecule so it can supply energy for movement to continue. The body re-synthesizes the ATP through different methods.

The Energy Systems

The body has three methods to produce ATP and therefore energy, and each method is referred to as 'an energy system'. One of these energy systems uses oxygen from the air: this is called the *aerobic system*. The remaining two systems can produce ATP without oxygen: these are called the anaerobic systems. The three systems are classified by the speed with which they produce energy. They are called the 'aerobic slow', the 'anaerobic medium' and the 'anaerobic fast' systems.

Aerobic Slow System

The aerobic system produces energy by synthesizing ATP through a series of chemical reactions involving oxygen. The system uses carbohydrates, fats and protein consumed from food to produce energy. The series of reactions that creates ATP from food can be thought of as the aerobic energy cycle.

The aerobic cycle is continually producing energy from our food sources. Which food source is used to produce energy is dependent upon the exercise intensity (the relative performance compared to maximum) and its duration.

Protein: Protein's contribution to exercise is very low, except during ultra-long distance events – for example marathon, iron man and so on – where it can account for a significant proportion of the energy.

Carbohydrates and fats: The contribution from carbohydrates and fats is affected by the exercise intensity: the greater the exercise intensity, the larger the contribution from carbohydrates, and vice versa.

At rest, the aerobic energy system produces the majority of its energy from fat and relatively little from carbohydrates. As the exercise intensity increases, the ratios switch round so that carbohydrates provide the majority of energy as compared to fats.

In addition to providing energy for low intensity exercise, the aerobic system is vital in the recovery process, as it removes the lactic acid that will have accumulated through engagement of the anaerobic medium system.

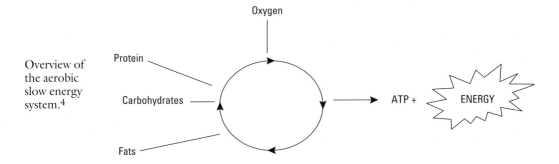

Overview of the aerobic slow energy system.[4]

The aerobic system is described as a slow system, due to the relative time it takes to produce energy. At higher intensities the energy is needed at a quicker rate, and to meet these demands the body begins to rely on the anaerobic systems.

Anaerobic Medium System

It is called the 'medium system' because it produces energy more quickly than the aerobic system, but more slowly than the anaerobic fast system. Energy is produced solely by using carbohydrates to synthesise the ATP molecule; this is achieved without oxygen, and produces lactic acid as a by-product.

The anaerobic medium system is used in two circumstances: it is called upon when the energy demand of an aerobic activity – for example, jogging – cannot be met solely by the aerobic system; and secondly, for providing the majority of the energy for high intensity efforts of 0–90sec in duration. The greater the intensity level, the more the anaerobic medium system is used.

Lactic acid: When the anaerobic medium system is called upon, the by-product known as lactic acid is produced, and builds up within the muscles to create a burning sensation. The presence of lactic acid interferes with the workings of the muscles resulting in less forceful contractions, decreased neuromuscu-

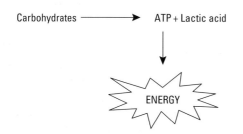

Carbohydrates ⟶ ATP + Lactic acid

ENERGY

Overview of the anaerobic medium system.[4]

lar co-ordination, and eventual cessation of the activity at that effort level.

The presence of lactic acid reduces the intensity level that can be maintained. When the body returns to an intensity level where the energy demand can be met solely by the aerobic energy system, the lactic acid is removed from the muscle through the circulating blood and a series of chemical reactions.

Lactate tolerance: The build-up of lactic acid alters the chemical environment of the muscles; consequently the muscles have difficulty contracting, and this results in performance at a lower exercise intensity level. Lactate tolerance refers to the ability of the muscles to contract forcefully despite the presence of lactic acid. It is an important attribute for rugby, as large amounts of lactic acid are produced during matches.

Certain training techniques will enable the body to adapt so that it produces less lactic acid at a given exercise intensity, and the muscles become more adept at functioning despite the presence of lactic acid.

Anaerobic Fast System

The fast anaerobic energy system provides energy immediately, and operates predominately for the first 0–10sec of exercise. The system delivers large amounts of energy quickly, though soon becomes exhausted and needs time to recover.

The system produces energy by using the substance creatine to quickly re-synthesize ATP from broken-down ADP. The amount of creatine in the muscle is limited. When the stores within the muscle become depleted, sufficient rest must be given to allow them to be replenished. It can take between 2–5min rest for the creatine to be fully re-synthesized to previous levels.

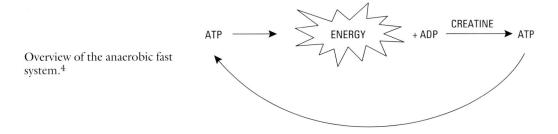

Overview of the anaerobic fast system.[4]

The small quantity of ATP already present in the muscle is used to give immediate energy. Then with the aid of creatine phosphate, it is restored back to ATP for further use to give more energy. The process is repeated until the creatine phosphate stores are too low to continue the cycle.

Interplay of the Three Energy Systems

If the qualities of the three energy systems are compared, it can be seen that the speed at which the energy is produced is inversely related to the amount of energy it gives: for example, the more quickly that ATP is produced, the less is made.

All three energy systems are working simultaneously, but certain systems dominate the energy contribution, depending on the situation. The duration of exercise is the major determinant as to which energy system dominates: the longer the duration, the lower the intensity level that can be sustained – for instance, you cannot maintain your 100m sprint speed for a mile run. The reason you cannot maintain the same intensity level is due to fatigue of the anaerobic energy systems. Although one energy system may be providing almost all the energy for a given activity, the other systems are still contributing small amounts of energy. Therefore each system is contributing to your performance throughout a rugby match.

Reasons for Fatigue

Fatigue can be defined as the inability to maintain an exercise intensity. The main causes for fatigue are as follows:

Depletion of an energy substrate: This refers to the exhaustion of the body's fuel sources, either from creatine phosphate or stored carbohydrates. The fat and protein stores represent an almost inexhaustible supply to the body. The depletion of stored carbohydrate is usually only seen in ultra-long distance events, such as a marathon. Creatine phosphate stores are depleted rapidly from high intensity exercise, and require around 2–5min to be replenished.

Lactic acid interference: The high demand of exercise can produce large amounts of lactic acid. The build-up of lactic acid interferes with the working of the muscles, resulting in less forceful contractions and therefore a decline in exercise performance.

Central nervous system fatigue (CNS fatigue): The signals from the brain to the muscles telling them to contract become weaker the more times they are required to be sent during an exercise session (though in the long term, the more repetitions that are performed, the greater the neuromuscular co-ordination). The body sends these weaker signals in an attempt to protect itself from injury, since the weaker signals result in less powerful contractions and therefore performance at a lower intensity level.

The effects of CNS fatigue would be seen if you were to do an upper body weight session after a game of touch rugby. The upper body muscles would be free from fatigue as they are not really used during the touch rugby. However, you would struggle to lift the same weights in the gym because the brain's signals that are telling the muscles to contract, are weaker from the fatigue induced by the game of touch.

CNS fatigue has an effect both immediately and in the short term. Immediate fatigue stops the body from performing the next sprint as quickly as the last; short-term fatigue means that the same training session may not be performed at an equal intensity if performed again the following day. It can take up to three days, and more, for the CNS to be fully back to its best from a demanding physical effort. The recovery process can be aided by performing very low intensity exercise on subsequent days.

When the body is continually given too great an exercise stimulus, the short-term fatigue of the system becomes prolonged, and lasts weeks to months. This is called overtraining.

THE FUNDAMENTALS OF PHYSICAL ABILITIES

When you watch rugby at the highest level, the abilities of certain players stand out from the rest: for example, Jason Robinson's ability to evade tacklers is almost unrivalled, while few can match the accuracy of Johnny Wilkinson's kicking. Athletes at the top of their game show amazing qualities that cover a range of different abilities.

In any sport, there are many physical abilities that are required to be successful; these vary from sport to sport and position to position. Different abilities can also prove successful even in the same position – for example the small, fast, agile winger may be just as effective as the strong, powerful, running winger.

When the qualities for a sport are analysed, individual players can be seen to have attributes that are classified under five broad categories; these can then be further subdivided into their individual components. The five main categories are:

- Metabolic conditioning.
- Strength.
- Speed and agility.
- Flexibility.
- Skill, technique and decision making.

Each of these areas is explained in the following section before applying them to Rugby Union.

Metabolic Conditioning

Metabolic conditioning refers to the ability of the energy systems to produce the necessary energy for a player to perform throughout the game. It can be divided into the main factors of aerobic power, anaerobic power and lactate tolerance.

Aerobic Power

Aerobic power is the ability to produce energy through the aerobic slow-energy system. As explained previously, the aerobic slow system predominantly supplies energy for exercise lasting over 90sec in duration, and is vital in the recovery process from repeated bouts of high intensity exercise.

A well developed aerobic slow system results in less lactic acid being produced at a given exercise intensity due to the reduced demand on the anaerobic medium system. The aerobic slow system has great importance in removing lactic acid from the body, because the greater the aerobic power, the more efficiently it can clear lactic acid and therefore allow exercise to be performed at a higher level.

Anaerobic Power

The ability of the anaerobic systems to produce energy is referred to as an athlete's anaerobic power. You will recall that anaerobic energy is produced in two ways: through the anaerobic fast system, which is the major contributor for the first 0–10sec of exercise; and through the anaerobic medium system, which supplies the majority of energy for the first 90sec. The system is also used in longer durations, where the demand for energy becomes too large for the aerobic system to handle alone. Intermittent bouts of high intensity exercise – for instance, repeated sprints with rests in between – also rely heavily on this system. Thus an athlete who has strong anaerobic power is able to sustain higher intensity levels and perform more intense sprints without suffering from undue fatigue.

Lactate Tolerance

As discussed earlier, lactic acid is the by-product of the chemical reactions within the anaerobic medium system. The build-up of lactic acid interferes with, and impairs, the muscles' ability to contract. Lactate tolerance is the main fatiguing factor for most team sports. Through correct training of this attribute the body adapts to functioning in the acidic environment, therefore resisting fatigue more efficiently during exercise.

Strength

Strength can be defined as the maximum force produced at a specific velocity (speed). This definition refers to the element of how quickly a force is applied. The speed with which a force is applied is an important yet often overlooked element of strength. Traditionally, strength is perceived as the ability to move the heaviest weight possible – although the force-velocity relationship states that this is just one aspect within the overall picture.

It can be seen that it takes around 0.8sec to produce maximum force: for instance, to lift the heaviest weight you can handle, or push as hard as possible in a scrum. Many movements in sport are performed in around 0.2sec or less – for example kicking, sprinting, passing, punching and so on. In this time scale there is not sufficient duration for maximum force to be applied: thus in sprinting the foot has left the floor after 0.2sec, therefore any strength produced after this point cannot be

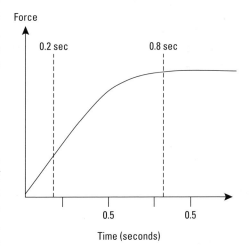

The relationship of force versus time. (Earlier versions of this can be seen by Steven S. Plisk.)[5]

used because the foot is in the air. The application of time-to-strength production means strength is classified as either slow-speed maximum strength (~0.8sec) or fast-speed strength (~0.2 sec).

Slow-Speed Strength

Slow-speed strength is also referred to as 'maximum strength', and is the maximum amount of force that can be produced: for example, the most force you can push with during a ruck or maul. This is an important aspect in rugby, where the player who holds the greater maximum strength will prove dominant in contact situations. The ability to produce maximum strength is related to muscle size – the greater the size of the muscles, the more force that can be produced – and neuromuscular co-ordination – the brain's abilities to recruit as many of the agonist muscles as possible, while relaxing the antagonist muscles to allow the movement.

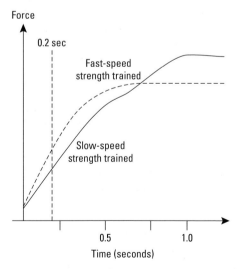

The effect of training methods on force production.
(Earlier versions of this can be seen by Steven S. Plisk.)[5, 6]

Fast-Speed Strength

Fast-speed strength, or just speed strength, is defined as the force produced at high velocities, in about 0.2sec or less. Training for speed strength increases the amount of force the athlete can produce within this 0.2sec time-frame.

The slow-speed strength-trained athlete produces less force within 0.2sec than the fast-speed strength-trained athlete, which would place him at a disadvantage during sprinting and other rapid movements. The ability to produce speed strength is dependent upon the following factors:

THE NUMBER OF FAST-TWITCH FIBRES: This is largely genetically determined, but through correct training techniques some muscle fibres will adopt fast-twitch muscle characteristics.

MAXIMUM STRENGTH: A certain percentage of the athlete's maximum strength is produced within 0.2sec, and through increasing the maximum strength, the force produced at the same percentage value will be higher: for example, if the athlete can produce 20 per cent of his maximum strength within 0.2sec, through increasing his maximum strength from 100kg (220lb) to 120kg (264lb), the fast-speed strength produced increases from 20kg (44lb – 20 per cent of 100kg) to 24kg (52lb – 20 per cent of 120kg).

NEUROMUSCULAR CO-ORDINATION: This describes the body's ability to co-ordinate the agonist, antagonists and stabilizers to produce a fast, efficient and forceful movement.

THE CONTRIBUTION OF THE STRETCH-SHORTENING CYCLE: The energy from the stretch-shortening cycle is a major factor in the amount of force produced in fast-speed strength movements.

Stretch-Shortening Cycle (SSC)

The stretch-shortening cycle (SSC) contributes extra force to speed strength movements. The SSC occurs whenever a muscle undergoes a rapid slight stretch followed by an immediate contraction from the stretched muscle. The cycle occurs in three stages:

1. *Stretch phase:* The muscles undergo a quick slight stretch.
2. *Pause phase:* The time between the end of the stretch (phase 2) and the beginning of the contraction (phase 3).
3. *Contraction phase*: The muscle undergoes a concentric contraction with more force than would be expected due to the SSC contribution.

During the stretch phase, the rapid slight stretch in the muscle(s) produces two responses. First, it invokes the stretch reflex of the body, a signal that tells the muscle to forcefully contract to protect itself from injury. This can be seen in the knee-jerk reaction where the knee suddenly moves from a slight tap just below the knee cap.

Secondly, during the stretching of the muscle, energy is stored, which then contributes to recoiling the muscle back to resting length: for example, the muscle acts like a spring being stretched. The two events result in additional energy contributing to the contraction, and therefore producing more force.

The effect of the stretch-shortening cycle can be seen by doing two vertical jump tests. In the first jump, squat down so that the thighs are parallel to the ground, then without moving any lower, jump upwards as high as possible. In the second jump, squat down to parallel, but before jumping upwards, quickly drop the thighs slightly below parallel, then immediately jump.

The second jump produces a greater height, as a result of the muscles in the thighs and buttocks invoking the SSC during the movement. This results in energy being stored, then used, and the stretch reflex making those muscles contract more forcefully, therefore producing a higher jump.

The stretch-shortening cycle only occurs if the pause phase – the time between the end of the stretch and the beginning of the contraction – is of a short duration. A long pause phase results in the stored energy being lost as heat, and the stretch reflex signal no longer being sent.

The SSC is involved in all running movements and most other speed strength movements, such as tackling an opponent, kicking and so on. Exercises that train the stretch-shortening cycle are called plyometric exercises.

Core Strength

This can be defined as the strength of the muscles around the mid-section that stabilize the hips and spine during movement. Strong core strength is essential to performance as it holds the body still, which allows full force transfer. For example, when tackling a player you hit them with your shoulder. A strong core would allow all the force in your legs to be transmitted through into your shoulder and on to the opponent. A weak core would not transmit anywhere near the same force, and you could see your own body buckle and collapse under the pressure, often resulting in a missed tackle.

The core muscles relate to, amongst others, the deep transverse abdominal (below the main abdominals) pelvic floor muscles (the muscles with which you can stop the passage of urine), the deep spinal muscles diaphram and the gluteus muscles (the buttocks). Through ensuring that these muscles are correctly working, then improving, their strength, the body builds a solid foundation upon which to increase the strength of your limbs.

Speed and Agility

Speed and agility represent different qualities, but are closely related. The different qualities are discussed below.

Speed

Speed, in its simplest terms, is the time it takes to cover a distance, and is a product of stride length and stride frequency. The winner over a certain distance is deemed the fastest: for example, the winner of the Olympic 100m final is deemed the fastest man/woman in the world. In rugby, as in other sports, speed is found to be more complex than it first appears, being made up of three different components:

Acceleration: The time it takes to go from a standing or slow speed to maximum or higher speed. It takes between 20–50m (65–164ft) to reach top speed, with élite Olympic sprinters attaining maximum speed at around 50m, while novices need just 20m[7]. The ability to accelerate is heavily influenced by leg strength.

Maximum speed is the maximum velocity (speed) that can be achieved. The maximum top speed displayed by an athlete is dependent upon neuromuscular co-ordination and the fast-speed strength of the legs.

Speed endurance: The ability to maintain maximum speed, or the ability to repeatedly perform successive sprints at the same speed. Speed endurance is dependent upon the metabolic conditioning of the anaerobic fast and medium systems.

Quickness: The ability to move a body part at the highest possible velocity. This is important in many sports such as boxing, racket sports or throwing events, where the speed with which the arms are moved has a large impact on performance. In rugby, quickness is important for passing and kicking the ball or in throwing a fake directional move, for instance a side step. It is closely related to the body's neuromuscular co-ordination and speed strength.

The three components of speed means you need different strengths, depending upon the distance being run; for instance, the winner of a 50m race will be the one with a greater acceleration, while the 200m favours those with a greater ability for speed endurance. Repeated sprint-speed endurance is important in team sports, as players are often required to sprint under conditions of fatigue.

Agility

Agility is the ability to explosively stop, change direction and accelerate again. It encompasses movements in non-linear directions – running backwards, in diagonal lines – as opposed to just straight line speed. Agility is a crucial requirement in rugby and most team sports, as movements are, more often than not, multi-directional. The player who can change his speed and direction the most effectively will more often than not prove superior. Agility is determined by the athlete's fast-speed strength in all movement directions, and the body's neuromuscular co-ordination of the muscles involved.

Flexibility

To function optimally, the body needs to have a certain level of flexibility. There are two aspects of flexibility: dynamic and static flexibility.

Dynamic Flexibility

This refers to the amount of movement you can actively produce around a joint. For optimal force production the body needs to be able to stretch to certain lengths so that the muscles are in an ideal position to produce the most force. A player's dynamic flexibility is influenced by static flexibility, and how warmed up the muscles are; for example, you would have better dynamic flexibility in the evening than the morning.

Static Flexibility

This can be defined as the range of movement around a joint – meaning the length the muscle can reach when slowly stretched. This influences your dynamic flexibility, and is essential for optimal performance and injury prevention. Injuries occur when there is an imbalance between opposing muscle groups, or muscles from side to side of the body; for instance, injury can occur from the hamstrings being tighter than the quads, or from the left hamstring being tighter than the right. Injury can be prevented by redressing these imbalances.

Skill, Technique and Decision Making

The skill of a rugby player includes, amongst others, kicking a ball accurately, correctly timing a pass, or choosing the right tactics throughout a match. These skills are developed through coaching and practice.

However, the ability to produce these skills and techniques, and to make correct decisions, is a function of fitness. When a tired player is asked to perform a routine action, the effects of fatigue alters the movement mechanics and thought processes. This results in a diminished ability to execute the skill and therefore a decreased on field perform-

ance. Through developing a solid fitness base the athlete will be better prepared to perform the required actions on the field throughout the duration of a match.

FUNDAMENTAL REQUIREMENTS OF A RUGBY PLAYER

The previous section outlined the physical characteristics that define an athlete. Rugby has a certain set of physical abilities that must be attained in order to achieve on-field success; although having said that, there is a degree of variance within these, as no two players are identical in their abilities, yet both can prove successful. This section outlines the major requirements a rugby player needs.

Through reviewing the demands of actual matches[8,9] the necessary traits a player needs to be successful can be seen. Analysis shows that in an average amateur club match there are different positional requirements. Distinctions in the game's demands can be seen between the inside and outside backs, and front five and back row. The author's experience has shown that players at club level are regularly asked to switch between the various positions within the Forwards or Backs. Therefore for the purpose of this book the requirements of rugby are discussed with regard to just the Backs and Forwards.

Forwards

The primary role of the Forwards is to secure possession from set pieces and subsequent phases. The Forwards must participate in scrums and line-outs, attempting to win possession of the ball and then track play to tackle the opposition or to secure their own ball. To fulfil these roles, the Forward must have certain physical attributes to be successful; these can be set out under the headings outlined in the previous section.

Metabolic Conditioning

On average a Forward covers between 4,000 to 4,500m per game, participating in over 100 rucks, mauls, line-outs and scrums. The average work:rest ratio is 1:1.4; this means that for every 10sec of high-intensity effort (sprinting, fast jogging or pushing in contact situations) there are 14sec of a lower intensity recovery (light jogging, walking or standing still). The large amount of high-intensity exercise performed requires a significant energy contribution from the anaerobic medium system.

In addition to this, the athlete needs a good level of aerobic conditioning to perform the exercise and aid in the recovery process. The involvement of the anaerobic medium system, coupled with insufficient rest periods, results in the build-up of lactic acid, and this places a high demand on the ability of lactate tolerance to allow successful on-field performance. The anaerobic fast system is used throughout the game, but is not a dominant factor as it is given insufficient time to fully replenish itself.

Strength

The maximum strength of a Forward is a determining factor in contact situations where the stronger athlete gains the advantage by being able to push his opponent backwards. In scrums, mauls and some rucks, the application of force is over a prolonged period of time, allowing the player to apply his full maximum strength. In making a tackle or attempting to break an opponent's tackle, it is the player's fast-speed strength that determines success, as there is insufficient time for maximum force to be produced. Fast-speed strength is also important in contact situations, as the player who applies his maximum strength in the shortest possible time gains the advantage. Outside contact situations, fast-speed strength is vital as it determines sprinting speed and the player's agility skills. Both fast- and slow-speed strength rely on sufficient core strength, and this is therefore a prerequisite for effective performance.

Speed and Agility

The average Forward will perform sprints or fast jogging over thirty times per game for an average distance of 17m (56ft) per effort. The short distances covered means that the ability to accelerate is crucial to determining success as opposed to maximum speed, which needs around 20m (65ft) or more to be reached. Repeated sprint-speed endurance is another quality important to the Forwards' game, as they are asked to perform over thirty sprints per game, often under conditions of fatigue. The ability to accelerate under fatiguing conditions can often be the deciding factor when facing a one-on-one situation.

On average, a Forward receives the ball 50 per cent of the time within 5m (16ft) of an opponent, which illustrates how they are used to taking the ball into contact situations. The presence of highly developed agility skills can allow the Forward to elude an opponent or effectively cover in defence. The ability to move in various directions as opposed to just straight-line running is another important attribute, as the average Forward participates in more than twenty non-linear movements – for instance lateral, diagonal or backward running – per game.

Summary

The Forwards need a highly developed anaerobic medium system with good aerobic power and lactate tolerance to sustain performance levels. They must have a high maximum strength to gain advantage in contact situations and to positively influence fast-speed strength. The ability to accelerate is a major influence on performance, while agility skills can give the Forward an extra edge during open play in both attack and defence. Underlying all the above abilities is possessing sufficient core strength and flexibility to optimize the above.

Backs

The role of the Backs is to use the ball when it is in their possession to score tries, and to prevent the opposition from achieving the same. Compared to Forwards they spend less time in contact situations as they are not involved with scrums or line-outs – even though they are still required to engage in rucks and mauls. The different roles lead to slightly different physical requirements.

Metabolic Conditioning

The Backs on average cover around 5,500m per game. The average work:recovery ratio is 1:2.7; this means that for every 10sec of high intensity exercise (sprinting, fast jogging or pushing in contact situations), they perform 27sec of low intensity recovery exercise, for instance walking, gentle jogging, standing still. The Backs have longer recovery periods in comparison to Forwards, but the peak amount of lactic acid produced at times during a game is equal to that of a Forward. This means that though the Backs have more time to recover over the course of the game, at certain times during play they work just as hard as the Forwards, producing the same large amounts of lactic acid. Therefore the Backs require a highly developed ability for lactate tolerance. The Backs cover more distance than Forwards, around 5,500m/game as compared to 4,000m–5,000m for a Forward, and the energy for this is provided by the aerobic and anaerobic medium system; it is therefore vital to have these energy systems highly trained. The anaerobic fast system is not a major contributor to performance due to the inadequate recovery periods, but it still plays a role in aiding energy for high intensity efforts throughout the game.

Strength

Due to the Backs not being involved in scrums or line-outs, they participate in considerably fewer contact situations as compared to a Forward. Despite this, it is still vital they win the rucks and mauls that they do enter. The ability to dominate in the mauls and some rucks is reliant on maximum slow-speed strength while tackling, and the majority of rucks are decided on fast-speed strength. To fulfil the Backs' primary roles they must rely on their speed and agility, which is influenced by their fast-speed strength. To positively influence this, the athlete needs to develop his maximum strength and the stretch-shortening cycle. Both fast- and slow-speed strength are reliant on sufficient core strength, and thus it is a prerequisite for effective performance.

Speed and Agility

The Backs perform in excess of fifty sprints or fast jogs per game for an average distance of 21m (67ft) per effort. The ability to accelerate is crucial to performance due to the short distances of most sprints, along with repeated sprint speed endurance. The maximum speed of a Back is rarely reached during a game, but when it is, it can be the decisive factor in those situations; for example, chasing a kick or intercepting a pass.

It is his agility skills that give the Back the ability to beat his opponent and create openings. Backs receive the ball more than 5m (16ft) away from an opponent 80 per cent of the time, and this allows him space to execute a move. His agility skills also allow him to cover effectively when in defence, as well as quickly covering ground during the seventy-plus non linear movements per game.

Summary

Backs require highly developed lactate tolerance in addition to high aerobic and anaerobic power. They must possess excellent agility skills, acceleration and repeated sprint-speed endurance. And the faster an athlete's maximum speed, the more it may prove advantageous in many situations. Underlying all these abilities is possessing sufficient core strength and flexibility to optimize the above.

The Implications for Training

It is important to note that both the Forwards and Backs require developed lactate tolerance, aerobic power and anaerobic power. They also both need excellent maximum strength and fast-speed strength. The more developed their capacity for speed and agility, the greater the benefit to performance. All players need sufficient core strength and flexibility to perform at their optimum. The similarity in requirements for the Forwards and Backs means the training programmes will also be similar, but for small, subtle differences.

THE FUNDAMENTALS OF TRAINING THEORY

The final part of this chapter looks into the basic theories and principles behind training, which will give you a greater understanding of why and how training programmes are designed.

Why Do Athletes Train?

A conditioning programme is followed to increase on-field performance. This is achieved by training the physical qualities that a player needs to succeed on the field of play. The improved physical qualities allow the player to fulfil their role more successfully. How much a physical quality can be developed is limited by the person's genetic potential – the highest level attainable by that person, which in turn depends upon individual genetics.

The Theory of Adaptation

The development of the players' physical abilities through training is explained by the theory of adaptation. When you are presented with a new exercise stimulus – for example, running two miles (3km), lifting an 80kg (176lb) weight – the body is shocked by what it experiences and reacts by changing itself so it can cope with such a stimulus if it is encountered again in the future: it changes the physical ability that was stressed during the exercise. For example, in response to jogging, increases occur in aerobic power; through lifting an 80kg weight, the body adapts by increasing strength and muscle size. This response to exercise is the underlying theory used in designing exercise programmes.

Once the body has become accustomed to the stimulus, it no longer increases its physical ability in response to that exercise routine; it is said to have reached a plateau. This is an undesirable stage, as our fitness attributes are no longer improving, despite our efforts; even though it hurts to do the exercise, you end up lifting the same weight, or completing the run in the same time.

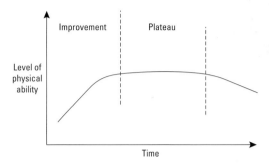

The response of a physical attribute to an exercise stimulus.
(Earlier versions of this diagram can be seen by Hans Sayle.)[10]

Progressive Overload

To avoid reaching a plateau, a technique called 'progressive overload' is used. The theory works by continually giving the body a progressively more difficult and challenging exercise stimulus, thus invoking it to continually respond by increasing the attributes stressed. The difficulty is increased through alterations of the training variables within an exercise programme, for example increasing the weight, decreasing rest, increasing the number of repetitions.

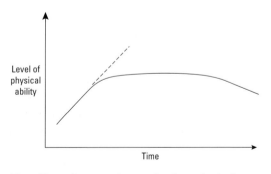

The effect of progressive overload on physical abilities.
(Earlier versions of this diagram can be seen by Hans Sayle.)[8]

The Law of Diminishing Returns

How much physical improvement can be expected to be seen from training is governed by the law of diminishing returns. This states that the closer you come to your genetic ceiling – your highest attainable level – the more difficult it becomes to increase your physical abilities, and the more effort in training must be applied to see improved performance. For example, a beginner to weight training could increase his strength by 33 per cent in three months, while an Olympic weightlifter may train all year to increase his strength by just 1–2 per cent. This means the more years you have trained, the smaller the gains you can expect to see from month to month.

Rest and Recovery

The often overlooked element of rest and recovery is every bit as important as the exercise you perform. It is not during a training session that your body improves its physical abilities, but over the following days after the session. It is therefore vital that you give the body the rest it needs; how long between each session is discussed in subsequent chapters, but it is important for you to listen to your own body language, which will tell you if the body needs more rest.

Overtraining

Overtraining is a negative state, where the athlete's performance level is decreased. It occurs from too much exercise without adequate rest, and the symptoms include decreased performance, altered mood states and persistent injuries. Recovery from overtraining may take several months if the symptoms are severe. It is avoided through ensuring that you take sufficient rest days, and plan a sensible exercise routine.

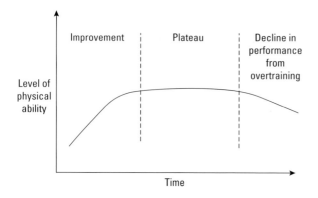

The effect of overtraining on performance.
(Earlier versions of this diagram can be seen by Hans Sayle.)[10]

Periodization

In recent years, the world over, the theory of periodization has developed into a science and now underlies all professional athletes' training programmes. The theory divides the training year into blocks of time using different training techniques at different stages of the year with planned periods of rest.

Periodization ensures that fitness gains are made continuously both weekly and yearly through correctly applying progressive overload to the training programme. The planned periods of rest are designed to avoid overtraining and decrease the chances of injuries.

Interference

This refers to the inhibitory effect one training method has on the other; for instance, long distance running diminishes explosive sprinting power. This means that a player is prevented from reaching his genetic potential in a physical attribute because of the effects of other training methods; for example, the same person could not be the fastest in the world at both 100m and 1,500m, as the two training methods would inhibit each other. The effect of interference is a consequence of training needs and is unavoidable for sports that require a variety of conflicting physical attributes, such as rugby and most team sports. Interference creates a ceiling of adaptation lower than that of the athlete's genetic potential; for example, the quickest rugby player in the world would have to change his training focus totally towards the 100m if he wanted to become the fastest sprinter in the world – and continuing rugby training would prevent him from attaining his full genetic potential in the 100m. In general, interference only really becomes an issue with full-time players at national and international level.

CHAPTER 2
Training Methodology

To improve your rugby performance all the physical qualities that are used during a game need to be maximized. Each one can be developed through training, though a variety of training methods must be used to ensure they are all covered. To help you in this, the interplay between the required physical qualities and different training methods is summarized below.

Using the six training methods described, all the required qualities for on-field performance are developed. You will note how flexibility and core training underlie the other five methods; this is because without adequate core strength and sufficient flexibility the other training methods will be undermined. The training methods use a unique combination of exercises, drills and routines to produce improvements in one or more of each physical quality. In this chapter we examine both the technique and the types of exercise used within each of the training methods.

This chapter should be used as a reference throughout the next twelve months. Return here periodically and review the information so you can be sure you have not developed any unwanted mistakes or forgotten any pertinent information.

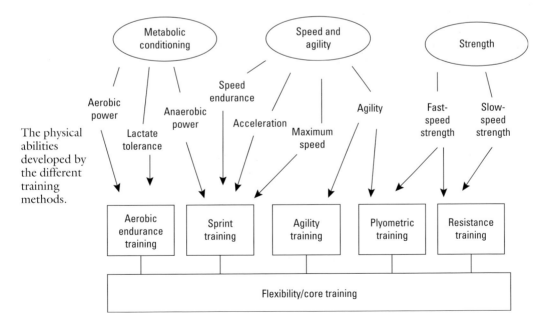

The physical abilities developed by the different training methods.

AEROBIC ENDURANCE TRAINING

The purpose of aerobic endurance training is to increase the athlete's aerobic power and his lactate tolerance. This increases the amount of energy produced by the aerobic slow system, and adapts the body so that it can continue to exercise despite the presence of lactic acid.

Running Technique

Aerobic endurance training uses jogging as the main mode of exercise, though it can employ other forms, for example swimming, cycling and suchlike. These do not produce the same on-field performance improvements, but they can prove effective alternatives when injury or the situation requires a substitute form of exercise. The jogging can be performed in different ways depending upon the training protocol, preferences and/or facilities. The different running types are described below.

Treadmill Running

This type of running exercise is performed indoors on a treadmill, and is an excellent technique that offers a controlled environment where alterations in speed can be closely and precisely monitored. The technique does not allow for changes in movement type. However, and some people find running indoors unnatural and tedious.

Lap Running

The jogging is performed by doing laps around an area, for instance jogging around a rugby field, athletics track or cricket oval. This is a good method because it allows increases in performance to be seen, as it is possible to measure accurately the distance covered during a run. The down side is that lap running can prove monotonous due to the unchanging scenery.

Road Running

Road running refers to the traditional running technique of going along roads or across country. This technique is excellent for providing variety in scenery, but it can inhibit interval training if a recovery period occurs when the route happens to be going up a hill.

Line Running

This technique is performed on a rugby pitch, whereby players run between the various lines, for instance the goal line to 22m. It is an excellent technique for mimicking the demands of actual play because it includes an acceleration/deceleration component.

Training Exercises

Even though aerobic training uses jogging, there are different types of aerobic exercise that you can perform in training. Each type of aerobic exercise uses one of the different running techniques described previously. The three main types of exercise used are described here.

Steady Pace

The athlete jogs at the same speed for the duration of the run. It is an effective method for developing basic levels of aerobic power, and to prepare the body for higher intensities in subsequent routines.

Interval Training

Interval training involves jogging fast for a set period of time, followed by a period of lower intensity, then a return to fast jogging. This process is repeated as required. Interval training can be further separated depending upon how you perform the lower intensity intervals, as described below.

Intervals with recovery: This technique involves running a succession of bouts at a fast jogging pace, interspersed with bouts of slow jogging to facilitate recovery. The athlete continues jogging for the whole session, but the speed he goes varies according to the structure of the intervals.

Intervals and rest: In this, the intervals of fast jogging are interspersed with periods of rest – meaning cessation of the activity, such as in standing still or a very gentle walk. The athlete therefore jogs maximally for a set duration of time, then stands still to allow himself to recover, before performing another all-out jog. Intervals with rest is a very challenging training method that greatly enhances both aerobic power and lactate tolerance.

The key element to be aware of during interval training is the length of the work periods compared to the recovery periods; this is the called the work:recovery ratio. The longer the recovery periods in relation to the work period, the higher the speed that can be sustained during that interval, and vice versa. The work:recovery ratio is more important than the actual duration of each high intensity bout. For example, a ratio of 1:1 could mean 60 seconds work and 60 seconds recovery, or 2 minutes work and 2 minutes recovery. Through manipulation of the ratio the athlete continues to develop his aerobic power and lactate tolerance without reaching a plateau.

Special Endurance

This routine is designed specifically to mimic the demands encountered in competitive matches. It uses a combination of movement speeds and movement types arranged in an order that reflects the exercise work-relief ratio encountered in a game.

The protocol has a slightly different design for Backs and Forwards to allow for the individual demands placed on them during a match. The training has the athlete either standing still, jogging gently, cruising (sprinting, but not at full speed) and doing full-out sprints. In addition to this the athlete performs lateral running and high intensity static exercise to mimic engagement in rucks and mauls.

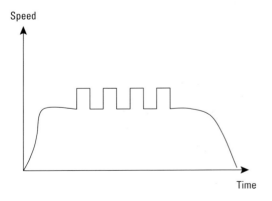

The variation of running speed during an intervals and recovery training session.

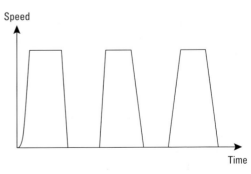

The variation of running speed during an intervals and rest training session.

SPRINT TRAINING

Sprint training improves the athlete's performance on the rugby pitch because it develops their acceleration, maximum speed and speed endurance. These components of speed are increased through the development of the fast and medium anaerobic systems, and by enhancing the body's neuromuscular co-ordination.

The training consists of sprinting distances ranging between 20 and 300 metres, with varying rest periods. The training can be performed on either an athletics track or around the perimeter of a rugby field, with the distances being estimated – for instance, 300m would equate to roughly two lengths and a width of a rugby pitch.

Sprinting Technique

The technique used when sprinting is an important component of running speed and performance. It is vital to focus on correct technique, and you should endeavour to implement the features described below if no particular style is present at the time.

Arm Action

The speed and power from running is greatly influenced by the way the arms are used: they should be vigorously pumped during sprinting, with the movement coming from the shoulder joint in a straight line as opposed to across the body.

Running on the Balls of the Feet

When jogging at slower speeds the heel of the foot is the first point of contact with the floor, serving to absorb the impact and improve running economy. When sprinting, using the heel to make the first contact with the ground acts as a brake and slows the runner down, so it is important to ensure that the balls of the feet make initial contact with the floor, pushing off to produce maximum sprinting speeds.

Relaxing

Perhaps the hardest thing to learn is the ability to stay relaxed, despite pumping the arms and moving as quickly as possible. When running, be aware of tension, and take care not to tense your face, fists and muscles, as this results in the whole body becoming tense and thereby inhibits your speed.

These skills can be developed by concentrating on correct technique during each sprint in the training sessions. Technique is also practised through the warm-up exercises that serve as sprinting technique drills.

Training Exercises

Sprint training is distinguished by the distances covered during the sessions. The range of distances that are used serves to stress the

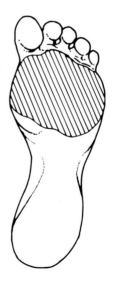

The area of the foot where ground contact is made.

different aspects of sprinting needed on the rugby pitch. A training session would normally focus on one particular set of distances using either 300m, 200m, 100m or a selection of distances from 0–60m.

The sessions are performed either on an athletics track or around the perimeter of a field, with the distances being estimated. It is necessary to re-emphasize here the importance of technique, and to say that sprinting technique should be practised and improved by using the sprinting drills as warm-up exercises before each training session, and by concentrating on correct mechanics during each sprint.

300m and 200m

These distances heavily tax the anaerobic medium system, producing large amounts of lactic acid. This enhances the player's lactate tolerance, thus allowing him to maintain running speed during times of fatigue.

100 and 0–60m

The shorter distances of up to 100m shift the focus on to the fast anaerobic energy system. Training for these enhances the athlete's acceleration and maximum speed, and the 100m also develops speed endurance. The development of these attributes is largely influenced by improvements in neuromuscular co-ordination.

AGILITY TRAINING

This training enhances the agility skills of a player – his ability to decelerate, change direction and accelerate again – and the training focuses on using movements in all directions. Agility training develops a player's neuromuscular co-ordination and speed strength, which results in an increased ability to change direction, speed, angle and movement type in all directions. Increased agility skills results in improved performance, as the player is proficient in one-on-one situations.

Agility Technique

Correct technique is vital in the production of an agile athlete. Technique should be developed during drills, with a concentrated effort made to ensure the following stylistic features.

Correct Use of the Head and Eyes

The head and eye position is integral to successful performance. The head and eyes should always face forwards, regardless of the direction you are moving in, unless focusing on an opponent or the ball. When turning from a back-pedal to forward running, the correct technique is for the head to turn first, with the eyes quickly focusing on a new point, then rotating the shoulders and the rest of the body. This initial head movement optimizes turning speed.

Arm Movement

The powerful arm action applied to sprinting is also important in agility. Vigorous arm action aids acceleration, turning and changing direction. There needs to be a conscious effort to use the arms while performing the drills.

Staying Relaxed

It is vital the player learns this difficult skill of staying relaxed while trying to move at high speed. Tensing of the face, shoulders and fists should be avoided.

In all agility drills it is important to concentrate on technique and control over speed

31

of movement. Once the technique has been mastered, the speed of the drill can be increased.

Training Exercises

The agility exercises use a variety of different movement drills, all of which are performed fatigue free to allow for effective practice of the technique. The agility training methodology is separated into different types of movement, which have varying degrees of complexity. The movements are described below.

Foundation Movements

These drills develop the foundation needed for multi-directional movement. The exercises are composed of simple, non-linear movements upon which more complicated and demanding exercises are based.

Basic Movements

The exercises combine the foundation movements to produce more advanced but still simple patterns. The protocol teaches the player simple transitions between movement types.

Combination Movements

The exercises develop more advanced movement patterns, the protocol focusing upon changes in speed, direction, and types of movement.

Rugby Specific Movements

The drills are designed to reproduce the forces and movements encountered during a game. The protocol includes some specific elements from the rugby field to prepare the player fully for competition.

PLYOMETRIC TRAINING[11, 12]

The purpose of plyometric training is to increase fast-speed strength through the contribution of the stretch-shortening cycle (SSC). The increased energy contribution by the SSC therefore improves performance in movements that are dependent upon this. Movements that are heavily influenced by speed strength include sprinting, changing direction, kicking, passing and suchlike.

Plyometric training uses various types of jump, either off one leg or two. The exercises are all performed at a fast speed with the emphasis on producing as much force in the shortest time possible.

Plyometric Technique

Unless the correct technique is used for the exercises, the plyometric response can be lost. You will recall that a plyometric exercise comprises three phases: the stretch, pause and contraction phase. The pause phase is crucial to exercise technique. If the pause phase is too long, the stored energy in the muscle is lost as heat and the body does not respond to the stretch reflex signal. The combination of this would result in no extra energy contribution to the movement and no improvement in the muscles' ability to use the stretch-shortening cycle. The pause phase can be kept short in duration by ensuring that all jumps occur immediately after landing. This will retain the plyometric nature of the exercise.

When performing the exercises, safety should be maintained by performing all training on a soft surface, for instance grass rather than concrete. However, a surface that is too soft results in an increased pause phase and possible loss of the plyometric nature of the exercise; therefore try to avoid excessively waterlogged pitches, and/or thick exercise mats.

On landing, the back should be straight with the shoulders in line with the knees, and the bodyweight distributed evenly on both legs.

Drill Intensity

Plyometric exercises can be very intense, creating large amounts of force through the muscles and joints. The exercises are classified as low, medium and high intensity, depending on the amount of force they generate through the joints. The medium and high intensity exercises are further classified into specific exercises, according to how much they replicate on-field movements.

The amount of force produced from the exercises is dictated by a variety of factors:

- *Type of jump:* Jumps on the spot create less stress than moving jumps.
- *Height of drill:* The higher you are jumping, the greater the stress on landing.
- *Speed of drill:* The quicker the movement, the more force is generated.
- *Weight of athlete:* A heavier athlete creates more stress to his joints.
- *Number of foot contacts:* Landing on one foot over two creates more stress.

For reasons of safety, high intensity exercises should only be performed when certain criteria can be met; the athlete should be able to perform:

- a three rep max of 1.5 × bodyweight in the squat;
- five squats in 5sec using a weight equal to 60 per cent of your bodyweight; for example, if you weigh 100kg (225lb), use a 60kg (130lb) weight to perform the five squats;
- the athlete should also have completed all the preceding exercise protocols during an off-season. Do not ever begin plyometrics using high intensity exercises; instead, lead

into them with lower intensity protocols first.

After following the above criteria you will be able to perform high intensity plyometric exercises safely, and reap maximum benefit. If, however, the athlete cannot, or has not, met these criteria, then medium intensity plyometrics should be performed until all the above have been achieved. Observing these guidelines decreases the chances of injury.

Training Exercises

Plyometric exercises are types of jump that engage the stretch-shortening cycle. The jumps are divided according to intensity. All plyometric exercises are performed for a low number of repetitions, with long rest periods to allow the muscles to perform free from fatigue, and therefore optimally enhancing the training response. Plyometric training is divided into low, medium and high intensity exercises:

Low intensity: These jumps are performed on the spot or over just 1m or 2m, using both legs for jumping and landing.

Medium intensity: These exercises introduce a series of jumps over longer distances, and more challenging jumps on the spot. Short sprints are added into some of the drills to replicate the sudden turn of speed encountered during matches.

High intensity: These exercises are performed on one leg, which greatly increases the stress placed upon the body. The exercises use a combination of jumps and hops, both on the spot or over a short distance. Some of the exercises include a sprinting component to re-create the demands encountered during matches.

RESISTANCE TRAINING

The objective of resistance training is to increase a player's muscle mass, fast-speed and slow-speed strength. A player's strength has a major influence upon performance, as it underlies speed, agility and success in contact situations. The development of muscle mass increases the athlete's weight, and can positively influence maximum strength. An additional benefit of resistance training is that the stronger muscles protect the joints and therefore decrease the chances of injury.

Resistance training involves performing an exercise using a weight, either bodyweight, as in a press-up, or with an external weight, such as a dumbbell. There are many exercises that work the body's different muscle groups, and these are performed for a set of repetitions: for example – 5, 10, or 15 lifts, followed by a rest period of, say, 30, 90, or 180sec. Through manipulation of the sets, reps, rest periods and the weight used, focus can be placed upon achieving the different benefits of resistance training.

Resistance Training Technique

Resistance training technique is concerned with the body position used during any of the exercises and the routines used.

Lifting Technique

It is vital that all weight-training exercises are performed using the correct lifting technique. Every exercise is described in detail in Chapter 3, with guidelines for correct techniques and commonly seen mistakes. Many people use a poor technique during an exercise. This is very negative in the long term, leading to stagnation at a certain weight, loss of flexibility and muscle weaknesses.

General Exercise Errors

In addition to specific errors seen in the individual exercises, there are other, more general mistakes made in the exercises, and these should be avoided.

Incomplete range of motion: This is the most common mistake seen in gyms. The exercise must be performed all the way from the beginning to the end, because failure to do so results in the muscles not being strengthened throughout the movement range. The main cause of this error is using a weight that is too heavy, thus forcing you to compromise your technique.

Extraneous movements: It is a mistake to move other body parts to progress the exercise; for example, leaning back when performing a biceps curl. Again, failure to achieve this correctly is caused by using too heavy a weight, or through lack of concentration when fatigue sets in.

Losing control of the exercise on the way down: When gravity is exerting its influence, for instance when you are lowering the bar downwards, you may risk losing control. An eccentric contraction is occurring to slow the speed at which the bar moves, and a conscious effort should be made to control the bar slowly downwards. This ensures that the muscles are worked both concentrically and eccentrically, giving much greater benefits. A general guideline would be to control the bar downwards in twice the time it takes to push it up.

Checking Exercise Technique

Even when you know exactly what you are doing, it is difficult to observe your technique while performing an exercise. To get optimal results it is essential to perform all the exercises with the correct technique. It is therefore suggested that you consult a trained exercise professional to monitor your movement patterns. This is especially important with anyone new to weight lifting.

Speed of Lifting

This refers to the speed with which the weight is moved during an exercise. It is vital that the bar is controlled downwards: this increases safety, as you are always in control of the weight and work the muscles in both directions, giving better results.

For the 'up' phase of the lift, when the most effort is required, the weight should always be lifted as quickly as possible. This ensures you are applying maximal force to the effort of lifting the weight. Although the exercise is performed by pushing quickly, when using heavy weights the bar may appear, to any neutral observer, to be moving very slowly. This is a consequence of using a heavy weight, but you should ensure that you, as the lifter, are producing the effort as quickly as possible, as this ultimately allows maximum force production.

As stated previously, as a general guide, look to control the bar/weight during the easy part of the lift by taking twice the time it took to push/pull the weight up during the hard part.

Point of Failure

The point of failure is the moment when you can no longer perform the exercise because of fatigue. The misconception is that *all* resistance exercise should be taken up to failure to achieve results. It is true that to increase muscle size (hypertrophy), the more frequently the point of failure is reached, the greater the expected results. To achieve the other training benefits – for example, to increase maximum strength and fast-speed strength – reaching the point of failure is not necessary, and the exercise should instead be stopped when you feel you can no longer achieve another repetition without the aid of someone else.

Lifting Order

The way the exercises are ordered has implications for the training adaptation that occurs. There are three general ways to structure the exercise order:

Consecutive muscle group exercises: The same muscle group is worked in consecutive exercise; for instance, to work the legs, perform the squat, lunge, then deadlift. This technique is used mainly for increasing muscle size (hypertrophy).

Alternative muscle group exercises: These are designed to allow longer rest periods for the muscle groups involved. After a muscle group is worked, a different muscle group is trained before returning to that initial muscle group; for example, do a set of squats, incline bench press, then another set of squats, then another incline bench press.

Circuit training: One set of each exercise in the programme is performed, then the circuit is repeated once more; for example: one set of deadlift, incline bench press, squat, bent over row, then repeat the circuit by performing one set of each once more. This technique gives the most rest between exercises, but can prove difficult to perform in a crowded gym where equipment is often busy.

Within each of the above exercise orders the following rules should be also be observed:

Large muscle groups before small muscle groups. The small muscle groups support the larger muscles in performing the exercises. If the smaller muscles are fatigued by doing exercises for them first, it inhibits fully targeting the larger muscles. This is because the smaller muscles reach their point of failure before the larger ones; for example, the triceps should be trained after the chest so that they don't limit performance in the bench press.

Power exercises first: Power exercises, such as jump squats, should be performed before other exercises so that fatigue does not affect performance.

Resistance Training Protocols

A training protocol refers to how the sets, reps, rest and intensity are structured, and to which exercises are used. These factors are designed so that the athlete increases either muscular size, or fast-speed or slow-speed strength. It is necessary to have different protocols as the individual benefits of resistance training cannot all be achieved to any great extent through just one. The protocols are discussed in depth later in the book, but the main types can be summarized as preparation, hypertrophy, slow-speed strength and fast-speed strength:

Preparation: This routine focuses upon preparing the player's body for future training. The techniques for each exercise can be mastered, while giving time for the tendons and ligaments to strengthen in preparation for the more demanding stresses to come.

Hypertrophy: Designed to increase the size of the muscles. The routine can be used to develop the size of all the muscles of the body, or to focus specifically upon the ones used on the rugby field.

Slow-speed strength: Focus is placed upon increasing the athlete's maximum slow-speed strength. The training protocol involves lifting high intensity (heavy) weights for a low number of repetitions. This type of training should only be performed by people who have been doing resistance training regularly for the previous two years. The heavy weight imposes a large stress on the body and this will cause injury unless you have strengthened the necessary tissues. To fully prepare the muscles, tendons and ligament to withstand these forces, a solid training experience of two years is required.

Fast-speed strength: The protocol increases the athlete's fast-speed strength. The training involves performing a low to moderate number of reps, but with lighter than maximal weights.

Resistance Training Exercises

There are many hundreds of exercises that can be used for resistance training, involving bodyweight and dumbbells through to resistance machines. The exercises test different areas of the body and are used at specific times of the year, depending on the training goal and routine. Which exercise to perform depends upon its specificity to the sport and on the training's goal.

Specificity

This refers to how much the exercise mimics the movements performed on the rugby field. An exercise of 'high specificity' is one that closely resembles the movement required on the field of play. A 'low specificity' exercise does not hold quite the same replication of on-field demands.

Where possible, choose the most specific exercises, but do not be too concerned if facilities force you to use an alternative of lower specificity, as many of the resistance training benefits come from the manipulation of rest, reps and intensity.

Alternative Exercises

Due to the large number of resistance exercises and the variations in facilities found within different gyms, each exercise has a number of possible alternatives to use. In an ideal world you would use the outlined exercises, but if that is not possible, choose from one of the alternative exercises given, focusing upon the most specific exercise available to you.

FLEXIBILITY AND CORE TRAINING

Flexibility and core training can be thought of as the foundation upon which all other training methods are built. Without adequate flexibility you cannot produce maximal amounts of force, and injury will always be lurking around the corner. Core training will strengthen the mid section allowing improved speed, agility and strength to be produced, and will also prevent injury.

Core training is a subdivision of resistance training, but its importance to performance is significant, which is why it is presented as a method in its own right. It is grouped with flexibility because these two functions are heavily reliant on each other. Tight muscles often result in faulty core functioning, and vice versa.

Flexibility Technique

Flexibility training addresses the length of the resting muscles, and the technique involves performing a series of stretch tests (*see* Chapter 4). Depending on these results, you can then pay extra attention to the stretches needed to elongate the tight muscles. Over time you will become aware of muscle tightness, and will know instinctively which muscles to focus on in your stretch routine.

Stretching Methods

There are a few techniques that can be used to stretch a muscle. The two main methods are:

1. Hold the stretch for 30sec at the point of mild discomfort.
2. Take the stretch to the point of mild discomfort, hold until the tightness disappears (20–40sec), then take the stretch to the next point of tightness, and repeat this process once more.

The second stretching method should be used to lengthen muscles, while the 30sec hold can be used to maintain the muscles at their current length.

Where and When to Stretch

Stretching can be performed after a training session, or at any point during the day – for instance while watching television, on the phone, sitting at your desk. To increase muscle lengths often takes a considerable amount of time, but by working the stretches into your life in the ways described above, adequate flexibility can soon be attained.

Flexibility Exercises

All the given stretches should be performed to maintain muscle lengths and prevent tightening from the effects of training. Which stretches you should pay particular attention to depends upon the results of the stretch tests. Each individual test has a desired point to reach, and failure to achieve this indicates the need to perform that stretch until the test can be successfully completed.

The tests should be carried out routinely in order to monitor flexibility levels. The length of a muscle is not a constant measure, with a large variation sometimes occurring from day to day. Tightness can develop from a tough training session, as a consequence of a match, or just from sitting for prolonged periods.

Core Strength Technique

The technique for core exercises is divided into two aspects. Firstly, it is vital to learn how to engage correctly the protective muscles of the mid-section. Once achieved, the focus is then placed on strengthening these muscles through various exercises.

Core Recruitment

To learn how to recruit the core muscles correctly you must first learn how to hold a neutral spine. This refers to standing with a correct posture, thus ensuring that all the joints are optimally aligned. To find your neutral spine:

- Stand with your heels, buttocks, shoulders and head against the wall.
- With one hand feel how much space there is in the arch of your lower back.
- A neutral spine should have just enough room for one hand to slide into the arch of the lower back while the heels, buttocks, shoulders and head remain touching the wall.
- If you cannot get your hand in the arch, or if there is room for much more than one hand – for instance, your fist – then your posture needs to be adjusted; this will come from following the stretches and strengthening exercises set out below.

Whenever possible try to reposition your body into the neutral spine position. This should be held for all exercises, and even when you are not exercising; for example when you are standing in a queue, sitting in the car, and so on.

In the neutral spine position you can then activate the core muscles. To do this you need to consciously:

- Contract the pelvic floor muscles, by stopping yourself going to the toilet at the back, then the front.
- Draw the stomach area below the belly button into the spine as closely as possible. Imagine you are trying to pull on a really tight pair of trousers and must get them over your lower stomach.

In addition to activating the core it is also necessary to use the larger muscles of the buttock and mid-section. To perform all the exercises, the larger muscles on the body must also be active along with the core so as to stabilize the joints. In all standing movements the buttocks need to be working, while the other muscles of the mid-section (abdominals, obliques) need to hold the mid-section stationary.

In all resistance exercises, but especially core exercises, it is essential to maintain a neutral spine and activate the core. It is easier to cheat both the exercise and yourself by losing correct spinal alignment or by not activating the deep core muscles.

Core Strength Exercises

The exercises to challenge the core involve a series of holds using your bodyweight and ideally a Swiss ball; the latter are now commonplace in all gyms, and easily obtainable through most sports retail outlets.

The exercises are each designed to challenge the body to gain core strength in each movement direction. The exercises are progressed through increasing their difficulty.

In addition to the specific core exercises, every movement involves the core and thus can act as a stimulus for increasing core strength. Therefore resistance exercises such as squats, deadlifts and cable twists are also great for developing your strength, as are other training methods such as agility or sprint training drills.

SUMMARY OF THE SIX TRAINING METHODS

The six training methods have been discussed, and the basic training techniques and routines within each method have been outlined. The use of these methods results in development of all the physical attributes needed on the rugby field. Through enhancement of these physical characteristics, higher levels of on-field performance can be consistently achieved.

CHAPTER 3
Training Exercises

This chapter is to be used as a reference throughout your training programme, as it contains descriptions for all the exercises used within each of the six training methods. I suggest that you look through this chapter only briefly when you are initially reading the book, but then constantly refer to the relevant exercises as you perform them during your training programme over the following twelve months. When to perform each exercise or protocol is discussed in detail in later chapters.

AEROBIC ENDURANCE TRAINING

This training method uses jogging as the mode of exercise; it can be performed in four ways:

Treadmill running	Using a treadmill.
Lap running	By doing laps around a rugby pitch, cricket oval, or suchlike.
Road running	Either along the roads or across country tracks.
Line running	Using the lines of the rugby field, and/or cones.

The relative benefits and drawbacks of each method were discussed in Chapter 2 (refer to that chapter if you are not sure which method to use). Aerobic endurance training has four main protocols: steady pace, intervals with recovery, intervals with rest, and special endurance.

Steady Pace

In this protocol the athlete performs a long, even-paced run, which is ideal for building a base of aerobic fitness.

TECHNIQUE:
- Road or lap running.
- Duration: 20–30min.
- Maintain an even pace for the entire period of the run.

COMMON MISTAKE:
- Going too slowly for most of the run, then sprinting at the end.

Intervals with Recovery

This uses a continuous run, with periods of quicker jogging, followed by slower jogging to allow recovery. It is a quite challenging training protocol that develops your aerobic base and trains the body's ability to deal with lactic acid.

TECHNIQUE:
- Road or lap running.
- Duration: 20min of intervals, 5min warm-up.

- Length of work interval: 1–3min.
- Length of recovery period: 1min.
- Number of work intervals: 5–10.
- After a warm-up of five minutes jogging, perform a series of intervals, running at a fast pace interspersed with periods of recovery, jogging at a slower pace.
- Throughout all work intervals use the same speed.
- Throughout all the recovery intervals use the same speed.

COMMON MISTAKES:
- Going too fast initially, thus being unable to perform the remaining intervals.
- Going too slowly on the first few intervals, leaving all the effort for the last one or two.

Intervals with Rest

A very challenging training protocol involving an all-out-effort jog, followed by total rest, then another all-out-effort jog. A great way to develop aerobic fitness and lactate tolerance.

TECHNIQUE:
- Road, lap or line running.
- Length of work interval: 6min.
- Length of rest period: 2–6min.
- Number of work intervals: 3.
- After a warm-up, perform a series of three intervals, running at a fast pace, interspersed with periods of rest (cessation of activity) for the prescribed duration.
- Perform each interval maximally while ensuring you are able to finish the required number of repetitions.

COMMON MISTAKES:
- Not completing the required number of intervals due to over-exertion in the first interval.

Special Endurance

This specially designed course is a great way to develop aerobic conditioning specific to a game situation.

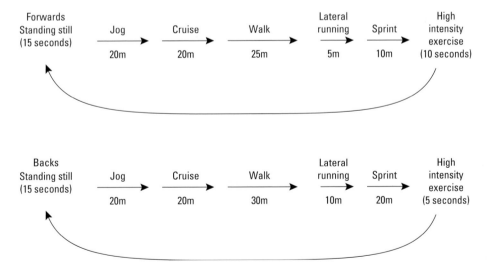

The special endurance training protocol.

TECHNIQUE:
- Line running.
- Number of repetitions: 20–40.
- Practise and learn the correct protocol for either the Forwards or Backs.
- Perform the prescribed number of repetitions.
- Ensure the lateral movement is performed facing the same direction so both sides are worked (left and right lateral movement) when going up and down the course.

COMMON MISTAKES:
- Not differentiating between different running speeds, e.g. jog, cruise.

SPRINT TRAINING

Sprint training uses distances from 20–300m. These can be performed on an athletics track or around the perimeter of a rugby field.

Sprinting Technique Drills

Sprinting technique drills are an important tool for developing your running mechanics and are used during the warm-up routine.

Fast Feet

The exercise is designed to increase your leg speed.

TECHNIQUE:
- Length/reps: 10m.
- Using small movements, try to get as many steps into the 10m as possible while ensuring you are pumping the arms with the correct action.

COMMON MISTAKES:
- Not keeping the head up and looking forward.

High Knees

The aim of the drill is to develop high and effective knee lift.

TECHNIQUE:
- Length/reps: 10m.
- While jogging, slowly exaggerate your leg movements so that the thighs are lifted parallel with the floor.

COMMON MISTAKES:
- Not using correct arm sprinting technique.

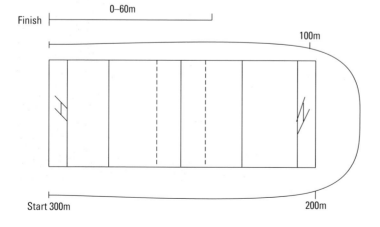

The distances covered during sprint training.

High knees technique drill.

High knees technique drill.

Arm Drill

This exercise teaches and develops powerful arm action.

TECHNIQUE:
- Length/reps: 30sec.
- Standing on the spot, pump the arms using correct running arm action.
- The body should be kept erect and the head looking up.
- The arms should go from hip to shoulder level in a straight line without any movement at the elbow joint.

COMMON MISTAKES:
- Arm motion not being from hip to shoulder.
- Arms coming across the body.
- Allowing movement at the elbow joint.
- Keeping the head down and looking into the ground.

Arm technique drill.

Wall Slide

An exercise aimed at increasing leg speed by decreasing the time between one foot contact and the other.

TECHNIQUE:
- Length/reps: 5 per leg.
- From a light jog, perform every third step by bringing your heel explosively into your buttocks without the foot going behind the line of the body.
- Perform five repetitions of bringing the right leg into your buttocks.
- Repeat with the other leg.

Wall slide technique drill.

COMMON MISTAKES:
- Allowing the foot to go behind the line of the body, so the exercise becomes more like butt kicks.

Butt Kicks

This drill develops high, powerful and effective leg bend during sprinting.

TECHNIQUE:
- Length/reps: 15m.
- Jogging slowly, bring your heels into your buttocks while pumping your arms.
- The emphasis should be on getting the heel to the buttocks as many times as possible in the 15m.

COMMON MISTAKES:
- Not using correct arm sprinting technique.

Butt kicks technique drill.

Pull-Throughs

The exercise is used to ensure the foot strike is both powerful and technically correct.

TECHNIQUE:
- Length/reps: 10 per leg.
- Standing on the spot, with a slight bend in the leg, bring it up to 90 degrees.
- Pull the leg down, focusing on striking the ground on the balls of the feet.
- Ensure the arms are pumping throughout using the correct arm technique.

COMMON MISTAKES:
- Lifting the legs over 90 degrees.
- Striking the ground with your heel.
- Not using the correct arm sprinting technique.
- Failing to get the thighs parallel to the ground with an almost straight leg shows tightness in the hamstrings or back that should be rectified through stretching.

Run-Throughs

These are submaximal sprints to focus on correct running action and to prepare the body for all-out sprinting.

TECHNIQUE:
- Run 60m focusing on correct running technique, but at a lower speed than with maximum effort.
- Gradually increase the speed of running with each run-through.

COMMON MISTAKES:
- Sprinting full pace on the first run-through.

Warm-Up Structure

The structure below shows how the sprinting technique drills are incorporated into the warm-up routine to ensure the body is adequately prepared for any training session. This routine should be performed before every training session and match:

- jog, 800m (two laps of the rugby field or athletics track);
- high knees, 2 × 15m;
- butt-kickers, 2 × 15m;
- pull-throughs, 10 each leg;
- arm drill, 2 × 30sec;
- wall slide, 2 × 5 each leg;
- fast feet, 2 × 10m;
- run-throughs, 2 × 60m (or more if you feel necessary).

Pull-throughs technique drill.

AGILITY TRAINING

The agility training exercises are divided into foundation, basic, combination and rugby specific movements. In all these exercises, markers can be used to set out the course. The markers can be from any objects that you have, or that are in the area, such as cones, rugby balls, clothes, litter.

Foundation Movements Agility Exercises

Lateral Movements

This drill develops the lateral movement running pattern.

TECHNIQUE:
• Length: 10–20m.
• With a slight crouch and the hands out in front.
• Move sideways, keeping the hips and shoulders facing forwards while avoiding crossing your legs.

COMMON MISTAKES:
• Twisting the hips and shoulders so that you are not moving completely sideways.
• Allowing the legs to cross over while moving.
• Changing the direction in which you are facing so that only one lateral movement direction is trained.

Back Pedal

The drill teaches correct backward-running technique.

TECHNIQUE:
• Length: 10–20m.
• With your weight forwards, pump the arms to aid propulsion backwards, while keeping your head over your feet.

Lateral movement agility drill.

Back-pedal agility drill.

46

COMMON MISTAKES:
- Leaning back so that balance is lost.
- Twisting so that the hips are not completely facing forwards.

Forward Diagonal Running

This exercise develops the ability to sprint at a diagonal angle.

TECHNIQUE:
- Length: 10–20m.

- Set out a square using the required length.
- With the hips and shoulders facing forwards at all times, propel the body diagonally from one corner of the square to the other.

COMMON MISTAKES:
- Twisting the hips, shoulders and head from facing forwards to the direction you are moving. Look at the accompanying photos to note how the body is facing forwards despite the direction the player is moving.

Forward diagonal running.

Backward Diagonal Running

This drill develops the often unnatural ability to sprint backwards at a diagonal angle.

TECHNIQUE:
- Length: 10–20m.
- Set out a square using the required distance.
- With the shoulders, hips and head facing forwards, move the body in a backward diagonal direction.

COMMON MISTAKES:
- Twisting the hips, head and shoulders so that you are performing more of a lateral movement or a pure straight line back pedal. Look at the accompanying photos to note how the body is facing forwards despite the direction the player is moving.

Backward diagonal running.

Schema of the weaving run agility exercise.

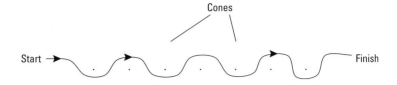

Cones

Start → Finish

Weaving run agility drill.

Basic Movements

Weaving Runs

The movement teaches you how to change direction gradually while sprinting forwards.

TECHNIQUE:
- Length: 20–30m.
- Using a 5m wide channel.
- Perform a weaving run while remaining forward facing, and ensuring you touch the sides of the channel every 5m.

COMMON MISTAKES:
- Not sticking to the 5m channel width.
- Failing to perform one width within the 5m.

Forward Zigzag Running

This exercise further develops your ability to sprint diagonally, and teaches you how to change direction while doing so.

TECHNIQUE:
- Length: 20–30m.
- Within a 5m channel.
- Forward diagonal running technique
- Move from one side of the channel to the other every 5m for the required distance.

COMMON MISTAKES:
- Losing the technique from the forward diagonal running.
- Not completing the runs within the 5m channel because running too fast.

Backward Zigzag Running

The exercise further develops your ability to sprint diagonally backwards, and teaches you how to change direction while doing so.

TECHNIQUE:
- Length: 20–30m.
- Within a 5m channel.
- Using backward diagonal running technique.
- Move from one side of the channel to the other every 5m for the required distance.

COMMON MISTAKES:
- Losing the technique from the backward diagonal running.
- Not completing the runs within the 5m channel, as going too fast.

49

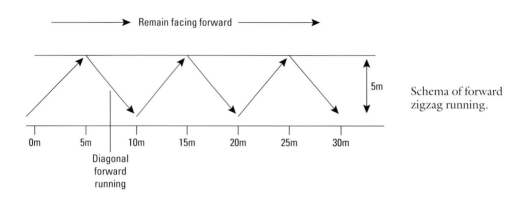

Remain facing forward

5m

Schema of forward
zigzag running.

0m   5m   10m   15m   20m   25m   30m

Diagonal
forward
running

Forward zigzag running.

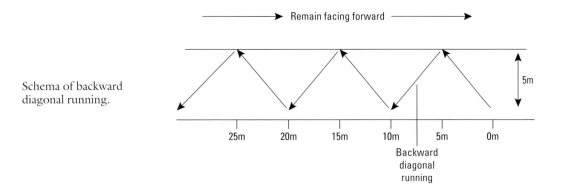

Schema of backward diagonal running.

Backward diagonal running.

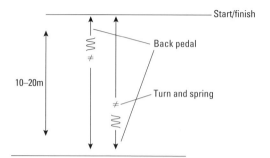

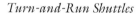

Schema of turn-and-run shuttles.

Turn-and-Run Shuttles

The exercise teaches you to accelerate and decelerate, and how to explosively rotate your body.

TECHNIQUE:
- Length: 10–20m.
- From a standing start, back pedal 3m, then turn as quickly as possible into a forward sprint.
- Stop at the next line, and again back pedal 3m before turning as quickly as possible into a forward sprint.
- Repeat for the required number of repetitions, turning to both your left and right sides.

COMMON MISTAKES:
- Turning only to the dominant side.
- Not leading the turning action with the head and shoulders.

Combination Movements Agility Exercises

Lateral Weaving Run

The exercise teaches and develops the ability to move using the different techniques, and to change between movement type.

Turn-and-run shuttle.

Schema for lateral
running agility exercise.

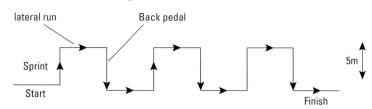

TECHNIQUE:
- Length: 20–30m
- Using a 5m channel, set out the course as shown.
- Perform a 5m sprint forwards.
- Move laterally for 5m.
- Back pedal for 5m.
- Continue the combination of movements as necessary for the required distance.

COMMON MISTAKES:
- Losing the correct technique from composite movements.
- Performing diagonal forward running instead of a lateral run.

Square Drill

The exercise trains lateral, forward and backward movements, and the ability to change from one to the other.

TECHNIQUE:
- Length of drill: 5–10m square
- Use lateral, backward and forward movements to cover the perimeter of the square.

COMMON MISTAKES:
- Losing the correct technique from the composite movements.

Diamond Drill

The drill trains diagonal forward and backward diagonal running, and the ability to change quickly from one to the other.

TECHNIQUE:
- Length of drill: 5–10m diamond shape
- Use diagonal forward and backward running to cover the perimeter of the diamond.

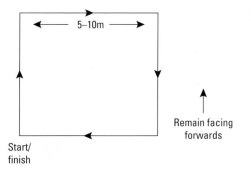

Schema of square drill.

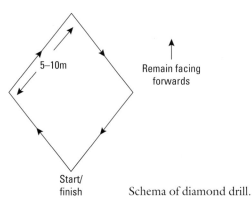

Schema of diamond drill.

COMMON MISTAKES:
- Losing the correct techniques from the individual movements.

Z-Pattern Run: Forward Running

The exercise teaches the body to perform high-speed changes of direction and movement type.

TECHNIQUE:
- Length: 25m–45m, 5 m wide.
- Use the composite movements to follow the course.

COMMON MISTAKES:
- Losing the correct techniques from the individual movements.

Rugby Movements Agility Exercises

Z-Pattern Run – Sideways Running

This drill teaches high speed transition from diagonal to lateral movements.

TECHNIQUE:
- Length: 25m–45m and 5 m wide.

- Use the composite movements to follow the course.

COMMON MISTAKES:
- Losing the correct techniques from the individual movements.

Forward Z–Pattern Run with Side Step

This run is designed to further develop high speed movement transitions, and introduces the skill of performing a side step before changing direction.

TECHNIQUE:
- Length: 25–45m, and 5m wide.
- With a rugby ball in hand and the course laid out as detailed below for a Z-pattern run . . .
- . . . perform the course facing forwards; at the end of each 5m forward sprint perform a fake side-step move to the opposite direction, before diagonally sprinting the other way.

COMMON MISTAKES:
- Losing the technique of forward diagonal running.

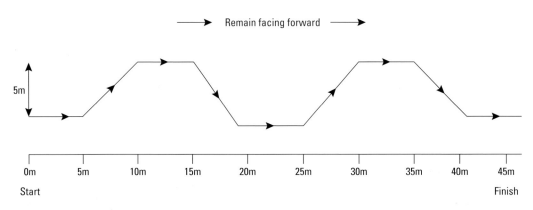

Schema of forward-facing Z-pattern runs.

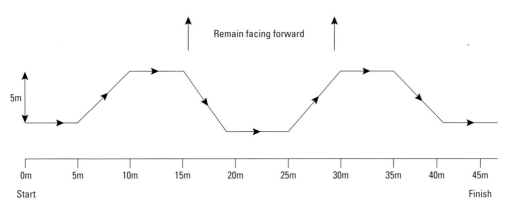

Schema of sideways-facing Z-pattern runs.

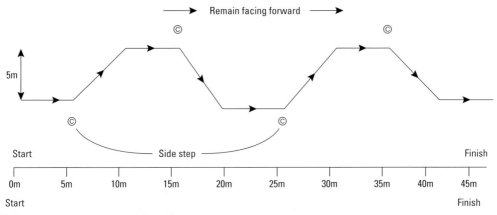

Schema of Z-pattern run with a side step.

- Failing to provide a convincing fake move, as too concentrated on completing the course.

Zigzag Running with Side Step

The drill teaches the player how to introduce a side step during a diagonal running pattern.

TECHNIQUE:
- Length: 25–45m.
- With the rugby ball in hand, and the course set out for zigzag running . . .
- . . . perform the diagonal running, but use a sudden side step to change direction on each corner into the next diagonal running segment.
- Change the hand used to carry the ball for the next repetition.

COMMON MISTAKES:
- Losing the diagonal running technique.
- Incorrectly performing the side step, and failing to produce a sudden change of direction.

The Cross-Agility Drill

The exercise teaches the player to accelerate and decelerate rapidly in lateral and linear movement directions.

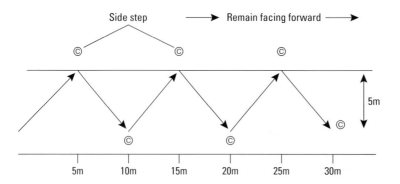

Schema of diagonal run with a side step.

TECHNIQUE:
- Length: 10–20m.
- Set out the course as shown, using markers on each end of the cross.
- Standing at the middle of the cross, sprint forwards to the marker.
- Back pedal to the middle point, and laterally shuffle to the right of the cross.
- Do a lateral shuffle back to the middle point, then back pedal to the marker.
- Sprint forwards to the middle point, and laterally shuffle to the left.
- Return to the start to complete the drill.

COMMON MISTAKES:
- Losing the techniques from the composite movements.
- Not returning to the middle point each time.

For all agility drills it should be remembered that technique is more important than speed of movement. Sacrificing technique for speed results in you adopting an incorrect movement pattern, and ultimately your true playing potential will be inhibited.

PLYOMETRIC TRAINING

Plyometrics are divided into low, medium and high intensity exercises, with rugby-specific

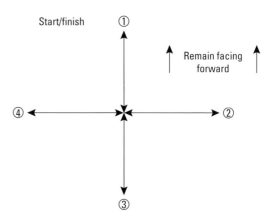

Schema of the cross-agility drill.

drills for the medium and high intensity protocols.

Low Intensity Plyometrics

Squat Jump

This exercise trains the muscles' ability to produce force with a two-legged pushing action.

TECHNIQUE:
- Assume a squat position.
- Jump upwards as high as possible.
- On landing, immediately jump again, and repeat for the required repetitions.

Squat jump.

COMMON MISTAKES:
- Not remaining in the same spot during the jumps.

Standing Long Jump

The drill trains the ability to produce and absorb maximal force quickly from a two-legged standing position.

TECHNIQUE:
- Standing with the feet together, jump as far forwards as possible.
- Upon landing, walk back to the start line and repeat the process for the required number of repetitions.

COMMON MISTAKES:
- Not jumping equally off both legs.

Lateral Jump

The jump focuses on the ability of the muscles to change direction rapidly while jumping laterally.

TECHNIQUE:
- Using a movable object that is knee height or below . . .
- . . . jump laterally over the object.
- Upon landing, immediately jump back to the other side and repeat for the required number of repetitions.

COMMON MISTAKES:
- Using an object that is too high: it should be of knee height.
- Using an immovable object, for example a wall, fence.

Standing long jump.

Lateral jump.

Note: The exercise can still be performed even if you do not have an object over which you can jump. Instead just use a line or article of clothing and ensure you are jumping above knee height.

Diagonal Jump

The exercise teaches the muscles to absorb the energy and use it to move the body diagonally.

TECHNIQUE:
- Standing with a small object to your front and right . . .
- . . . jump diagonally forwards to the right and over the object.
- On landing, immediately jump back to the starting position, and repeat continuously for the required number of repetitions.
- Ensure your hips remain facing forwards so that a diagonal jump is performed, and not a forward jump.

- On the next set, jump in the other direction, diagonally to the left and back.

COMMON MISTAKES:
- Using a fixed object.
- Using an object that is above knee height.
- Allowing the hips to twist so you are performing a forward jump.

Medium Intensity Plyometrics

Split-Squat Jump

The drill trains the muscles to produce force with the legs in a split stance position.

TECHNIQUE:
- With one foot in front of the other, jump upwards as high as possible.
- Land with the feet in the same position and jump upwards immediately upon touching the ground.
- After one set of repetitions, change the leg position around for the next set.

Diagonal jump.

Split-squat jump.

COMMON MISTAKES:
Going too low on landing and losing the plyometric nature of the exercise.

Double-Leg Hop

The exercise teaches the body to absorb and use energy from a jumping action.

TECHNIQUE:
- With your feet together, jump equally off both legs.
- On landing, immediately jump forwards again and repeat for the required number of repetitions.

COMMON MISTAKES:
- Losing balance from jumping too quickly.
- Not jumping equally off both legs, instead favouring the dominant side.

Double-Leg Zigzag Hop

The drill adapts the body into using energy from jumping in a diagonal forward direction.

TECHNIQUE:
- Standing alongside a line of objects (or just a line if no objects are available).
- Jump diagonally forwards and over the line.
- Upon landing, jump diagonally back over the line of cones, and repeat for the required number of jumps.

COMMON MISTAKES:
- Using an immovable object or an object that is too high.

Sideways Hopping

The exercise forces the body to learn to control the forces produced when successively jumping in the same lateral direction.

Double-leg hop.

Double-leg zigzag hop.

TECHNIQUE:
- With the hips facing forwards, jump laterally to the right.
- Jump again in the same direction immediately upon landing, and continue for the required number of jumps.
- Repeat the next set jumping in the opposite direction.

COMMON MISTAKES:
- Allowing hips to twist from facing forwards.

BELOW: Sideways hopping.

Medium Intensity Specific Drills

Cycled Split-Squat Jump with Movement

This advanced exercise teaches the muscles to use the stretch-shortening reflex in a similar manner to sprinting.

TECHNIQUE:
- Assuming a split-squat stance . . .
- . . . jump forwards as high and as far as possible.
- While in the air, alternate the position of the legs.
- On landing, jump again, switching the legs in mid-air once more . . .
- . . . and repeat for the required number of repetitions.

COMMON MISTAKES:
- Going too low on landing and losing the plyometric nature of the exercise.

Double-Leg Hop with 15m Lateral Movement Run

The exercise further continues to develop the ability to utilize energy while jumping, but includes an agility and sprinting component.

TECHNIQUE:
- Perform the required double-leg hops as set out previously.
- Upon landing from the final jump, immediately break into a lateral movement run to the left for 15m.
- In the next set, repeat with a 15m lateral movement to the right.

COMMON MISTAKES:
- Not turning sharply at a 90-degree angle to move laterally.

Cycled split-squat jump with movement.

Double-leg hop with 15m lateral movement run.

Double-Leg Zigzag Hop and 15m Forward Sprint

The exercise further develops the ability to jump diagonally forwards and also the ability to break into a forceful sprint from such a movement.

TECHNIQUE:
- Perform the required number of zigzag hops.
- Upon landing from the final jump, immediately sprint 15m forwards.

COMMON MISTAKES:
- Losing correct sprint mechanics.

Lateral Jump with 15m Turn and Sprint

The exercise teaches the muscles how to change direction in a sideways movement plane while including a turn-and-sprint agility component at the end.

TECHNIQUE:
- Perform the lateral jump for the required number of repetitions.
- Upon landing on the final jump, immediately perform a 180-degree turn, and sprint 15m.
- Repeat for the next set turning in the other direction.

COMMON MISTAKES:
- Turning only to the dominant side.
- Initiating the turn before landing from the final jump.

Double-leg zigzag hop and 15m forward sprint.

Lateral jump with 15m turn and sprint.

High Intensity Plyometrics

Single-Leg Squat Jump

This drill develops the single-leg strength to absorb and utilize energy in a jumping action.

TECHNIQUE:
- From a standing start, use just one leg to jump vertically as high as possible.
- Upon landing, immediately jump upwards again, and repeat for the required repetitions.
- On the next set, repeat using the other leg.

COMMON MISTAKES:
- Not remaining in the same place throughout the set.

Single-Arm Bound

The exercise trains the muscles to improve their ability to use the stretch-shortening cycle during the sprinting action.

TECHNIQUE:
- Length: 25m–45m.
- Perform an exaggerated running technique where each stride is instead a jump, with emphasis on height and distance per stride.
- Begin with a slight jog before breaking into the bound by exaggerating your running action through jumping.

COMMON MISTAKES:
- Emphasizing speed of movement over height and distance.
- Not using correct arm sprinting technique.

Single-Leg Zigzag Hop

The exercise trains the body to change direction while on one leg in a diagonal plane.

TECHNIQUE:
- Perform the exercise as set out in the double-leg zigzag hop, but use only one

Single-leg squat jump.

leg. Complete the required repetitions on the one leg, then repeat using the other.

COMMON MISTAKES:
• Using an immovable object.

Single-arm bound.

Single-Leg Lateral Jump

The drill develops the strength to change direction using one leg in a lateral plane.

TECHNIQUE:
• Standing to the side of an object . . .
• . . . use one leg to jump sideways over it.
• When landing on the other side, immediately jump back to where the exercise began.
• Jump continuously off one leg for the required repetitions.
• Repeat with other leg.

COMMON MISTAKES:
• Using an immovable object.

High Intensity Specific Plyometrics

Single-Leg Hop + 15m Lateral Movement to the Side

The exercise teaches the body to handle the stress of jumping and landing on one leg, while adding an agility component to move laterally at the end of the exercise.

Single-leg zigzag hop.

67

Single-leg lateral jump.

TECHNIQUE:
- Perform the required number of hops by jumping off from, and landing on, the same leg.
- On landing from the final hop, immediately perform a lateral movement 15m to the left.
- Repeat using the other leg, and laterally sprint to the right instead of the left.

COMMON MISTAKES:
- Losing control of the hopping, as moving too fast.
- Sprinting before landing from the final hop.

Double-Arm Bound

This exercise is an advanced version of the single-arm bound. The double-arm action produces more force, and thus poses a greater stress on the leg musculature in this sprinting-specific exercise.

TECHNIQUE:
- Length: 25–45m
- Jog into the exercise, then begin the exaggerated running action by . . .
- . . . jumping instead of striding.
- Use both arms to give momentum to each stride by forcefully propelling the arms backwards and forwards.

COMMON MISTAKES:
- Not performing the bound in a straight line as balance is lost.

Single-Leg Zigzag Hop and 15m Forward Sprint

The exercise challenges the muscles to diagonally change direction before rapidly sprinting forwards.

TECHNIQUE:
- Perform the required number of zigzag hops on one leg only.

Single-leg hop + 15m lateral movement to the side.   Double-arm bound.

Single-leg zigzag hop and 15m forward sprint.

- On landing from the final hop, sprint 15m forwards.
- Repeat with the other leg.

COMMON MISTAKES:
- Using an immovable object.

Single-Leg Lateral Jump with 15m Turn and Sprint

The exercise demands the body to produce force rapidly to change lateral direction before forcefully turning and sprinting.

TECHNIQUE:
- Perform the required number of single-leg lateral hops.
- On landing from the final hop, immediately turn through 180 degrees, and sprint 15m.
- Repeat using the other leg, and ensure that you turn in both directions.

COMMON MISTAKES:
- Only turning to your dominant side.
- Using a fixed object.

RESISTANCE EXERCISES

The following section gives step-by-step instructions, and identifies mistakes commonly encountered during resistance training exercises.

Squat

The squat develops strength in the thighs, buttocks, back and core muscles. It can prove a difficult exercise to perform if you have trouble with your flexibility.

TECHNIQUE:
- With the bar comfortably across your shoulders . . .

Single-leg lateral jump with 15m turn and sprint.

- Keep the back straight and the heels on the floor, then slowly move downwards until the thighs are parallel with the floor.
- Keep the knees over the feet throughout the exercise and do not take the thighs lower than the point where the back rounds or the heels come off the floor.
- If the thighs can reach parallel with true technique, push upwards back to the starting position.

COMMON MISTAKES:
- Not lowering the thighs to 90 degrees. If technique is lost before this point you need to work on your flexibility. Through stretching of the calves, hamstrings, hips and chest, and mobilizing the spine over time, you will be able to do the exercise throughout the desired range of motion.
- Allowing the thighs to go below parallel.
- Letting the knees move excessively past the feet.
- Losing the straight spine so that the back is rounded.

ALTERNATIVE EXERCISES:
- Deadlift, Smith machine squat, one-legged squats, leg press.

Straight-Leg Deadlift

This exercise develops the strength of the hamstrings, back and core musculature.

TECHNIQUE:
- With a slightly wider-than-shoulder-width grip on the bar, and a slight bend in the knees . . .
- . . . slowly lower the bar straight downwards without bending the knees and while keeping the back straight.
- Only go to mid-shin level or less if flexibility is limiting.
- Return to the start position and repeat.

71

Squat.

Straight-leg deadlift.

COMMON MISTAKES:
- Rounding the back.
- Allowing movement at the knees, therefore making this similar to the squat or a standard deadlift.
- Holding the legs completely straight.
- Going too low and over-stretching the hamstrings.

ALTERNATIVES:
- Squat, leg press, reverse leg press.

Jump Squat

A great developer of explosive power, the exercise greatly improves the fast-speed strength of the legs.

TECHNIQUE:
- Holding dumb-bells, squat down until the thighs are parallel with the floor.
- After a slight pause, jump explosively upwards as high as possible.

- On landing, pause before slowly lowering yourself back to the starting position and repeating.

COMMON MISTAKES:
- Not pausing between reps so the exercise becomes like the plyometric exercise of squat jumps.

ALTERNATIVES:
- Use a bar instead of dumb-bells.

Lunge

The lunge is a fantastic exercise to develop co-ordination, leg strength and core stability.

TECHNIQUE:
- Standing with the feet together using dumb-bells or a barbell, take a larger-than-average step forwards.
- Control the movement so that the back knee is 1in from the floor.

Jump squat.

73

- Powerfully push back to beginning position.
- Repeat the next repetition using the other leg to step forwards.

COMMON MISTAKES:
- Allowing the knee to shoot forwards over the front foot.
- Allowing the front heel to leave the ground.

ALTERNATIVES:
- Step-ups, one-legged squats.

Dumb-bell (Barbell) Incline Press

This exercise develops the pushing muscles of the chest, shoulders and arms. It is preferred over the flat bench press as it requires the muscles to be used at an angle more often encountered during matches.

TECHNIQUE:
- With the bench at a slight angle (30 degrees) and the dumb-bells touching the chest . . .
- . . . straighten the arms directly upwards, while *avoiding* forcefully locking out the elbows.

COMMON MISTAKES:
- Allowing the dumb-bells to move together or outwards from the body.

ALTERNATIVES:
- Barbell incline, Smith machine incline, flat bench press, seated chest press.

Standing Dumb-Bell Shoulder Press

Develops both the shoulders and arms as well as providing a challenge to the core muscles.

Lunge.

TECHNIQUE:
- Standing with a neutral spine, have the dumb-bells touching the front of the shoulders.
- Push upwards, keeping the elbows under the wrists.

COMMON MISTAKES:
- Allowing the arms to rotate so that the elbows are not under the wrists. This is indicative of shoulder tightness and the need to perform the chest stretch.
- Not pushing directly upwards.

Incline bench press.

Shoulder press.

ALTERNATIVES:
- Shoulder press machine, barbell shoulder press, Smith machine press.

Bent Over Row

A great exercise to develop the strength of the upper back while also demanding stabilization work from the core and lower back.

TECHNIQUE:
- With a shoulder-width grip, bend from the waist down to 60 degrees while maintaining a straight back.
- Pull the bar along the thighs into the hips.
- Squeeze the shoulder blades together at the top of the pull.

COMMON MISTAKES:
- Losing the straight back.
- Standing too upright and losing the 60-degree angle.
- Pulling the bar straight upwards instead of along the thighs.

ALTERNATIVES:
- Dumb-bell bent over row, one-armed bent over row, low row, seated row, T-bar row.

Chin-Ups

The exercise develops the pulling muscles of the back and arms.

TECHNIQUE:
- With your hands facing yourself, keep the torso erect.
- Pull the elbows down until the bar reaches the upper chest.

COMMON MISTAKES:
- Pulling with the whole upper body to produce the movement.

ALTERNATIVES:
- Lateral pulldown, bent over row, body-weight chins.

Bent over row.

Cable Twist

The cable twist focuses on, and develops, the muscles used to rotate the spine.

TECHNIQUE:
- Standing side-on to the cable, hold the handle with fingers interlocked.
- Begin squatting down while simultaneously twisting the mid-section until the hands are outside the knee.
- Repeat facing the other direction after completing the required number of reps.

COMMON MISTAKE:
- Bending the arms too much so they perform most of the work during the exercise instead of the muscles of the mid-section.

ALTERNATIVES:
- Ball twist, medicine ball side pass.

Push and Pull

The exercise demands that the body learns to stabilize itself against the forces produced by the arms when lifting the weights.

TECHNIQUE:
- With the feet shoulder-width apart, hold the cables with arms at shoulder height.
- Simultaneously push and pull, while keeping the mid-section rigid.
- Repeat facing the other way after the required repetitions.

COMMON MISTAKE:
- Allowing the body to twist during the exercise.
- Allowing the arms to drop below shoulder level.

ALTERNATIVES:
- One-armed cable push-and-pull exercises.

Chin-ups.

Cable twist.

Ball Crunch

The crunch is used to strengthen the stomach muscles, the ball providing an extra demand on the core muscles. It is important to learn how to get the abdominals really working during each repetition, thus avoiding having to do hundreds of reps. The abdominals are the same as any other muscles, and should be trained in the same manner as you would your chest or thighs.

TECHNIQUE:
• With arms by the head, knees bent and the lower back resting on the ball . . .
• . . . pull the chest upwards as high as possible while keeping the lower back in contact with the ball; ensure you are not using the legs.

PROGRESSION:
• Addition of weight to the chest.

COMMON MISTAKE:
• Using the legs and arms to generate momentum.

ALTERNATIVES:
• Various abdominal exercises.

Back Raises

The exercise builds the back muscles either side of the spine and engages the hamstrings and buttock.

TECHNIQUE:
• Perform this exercise on a back extension machine or ball.
• Lower the body as low as possible.
• Return to start position and repeat.

PROGRESSION:
• Holding a weight to the chest.

Push and
pull.

Ball crunch.

Back raises.

COMMON MISTAKE:
* Using the legs and arms to generate momentum.

ALTERNATIVE:
* Four-point back-raise exercise.

Alternative Exercises

If you are unable to use any exercise outlined previously, choose an appropriate alternative from the list provided. When deciding which alternative to use, try and pick the next most specific exercise, as detailed in Table 1 opposite.

CORE TRAINING AND FLEXIBILITY

Within all these exercises, for both flexibility and core strength it is important to remember to hold a neutral spine and to recruit the core. To do this you must learn what a neutral spine feels like, and then practise recruiting the muscles.

TABLE 1: RANKING OF RESISTANCE EXERCISES ACCORDING TO SPECIFICITY

Target area	Exercises	Order of specificity
Legs	Step-ups One-legged squats Reverse leg press Smith machine squats Leg press Leg extension Leg curl Calf raises	High ↓ Low
Upper body – Pushing	One-armed push Flat bench press Seated shoulder press Dips Lateral raise Triceps pulldown	High ↓ Low
Upper body – Pulling	One-armed pulls Low row Seated machine row T-bar row Biceps curls	High ↓ Low
Trunk	Medicine ball pass Four point back raises Various abdominal exercises	High ↓ Low

Core Conditioning Training

Prone Ball Hold

This exercise develops the core muscles in the prone lying position. Ensure you are maintaining a neutral spine, as any deviation from this reduces the difficulty and the effectiveness of the exercise.

TECHNIQUE:
- Lie face down on the ball, and roll out to an appropriate length.
- Ensure the arms are directly below the body and that you have a neutral spine.
- Maintain the position until the desired time is achieved, or you are unable to maintain your neutral spine any longer.
- Difficulty is increased by having less of your body on the ball. Once you are at your feet, go back to the beginning, but use just one arm only on the floor.

COMMON MISTAKE:
- Continuing to hold the position despite losing the neutral spine.

Prone ball hold.

Alternative:
Plank on the floor without a ball.

Side-Lying Ball Hold

This exercise focuses upon the stabilizer muscles in the sides.

Side-lying ball hold.

TECHNIQUE:
- With the feet against the wall, ensure your body has a straight neutral spine alignment.
- Hold the position until you complete the desired time, or lose your neutral spine.
- Increase the difficulty by resting on the ball further down your leg. The exercise can also be made more demanding by holding the arms by the head, or holding a weight to the chest.

COMMON MISTAKE:
- Losing the neutral spine, especially the head being out of alignment.

ALTERNATIVE:
- Side lying floor plank.

Supine Ball Bridge

This exercise develops the strength, balance and co-ordination of the hamstrings, buttocks and core muscles.

TECHNIQUE:
- Lying on your back with your feet on the ball, assume a neutral spine position.
- Hold until the neutral spine is lost, or the desired time is completed.
- Increase the difficulty by performing on one leg. Once mastered, introduce a curl movement by straightening and bending the leg.

COMMON MISTAKE:
- Using the arms on the floor to balance.

ALTERNATIVE:
- Supine floor bridge.

Double-leg supine ball bridge.

Single-leg supine ball bridge.

Ball Twist

The exercise develops the muscles used to rotate the body, primarily the obliques. It needs a certain degree of flexibility for optimal effectiveness, therefore focus on the relevant stretches if you are not able to perform this at first.

TECHNIQUE:
- With the head and shoulders on the ball, and the body horizontal with a neutral spine alignment, . . .
- . . . rotate 90 degrees in one direction, then rotate through to the same position facing the other way.
- Repeat as required.
- Increase the difficulty by holding a dumbbell in your hands. This weight can then be increased when appropriate.

COMMON MISTAKE:
- Allowing the whole body to move from side to side, rather than just twisting on the spot. This is a sign of inflexibility, and focus should be placed on the back twist stretch, amongst others.

ALTERNATIVE:
- Medicine ball side pass.

Ball twist.

Flexibility Training

Try to focus on the muscles that are deemed tight from the stretch tests in Chapter 4. However, during all these exercises it is important to sense tightness from side to side of the body, and to focus on the tighter areas. Flexibility can change significantly from day to day. You should be looking out for muscles that have tightened, even if they passed the stretch tests. Therefore perform all the stretches regularly, but spend extra time on the muscles you know are tight.

Neck Side and Neck Twist Stretches

This is an excellent pair of stretches to ensure that the neck is loose, and has equal flexibility from side to side.

TECHNIQUE:

- While standing or sitting down on a bench, keep your shoulders down, and the back in a neutral spine alignment.
- With your free hand, tilt your head to this side.
- Then rotate your head to the side.
- Repeat, stretching the neck in the other direction.

COMMON MISTAKES:

- Being too aggressive with the stretch.
- Allowing the body to lean over as you stretch.

ALTERNATIVES: N/a.

Neck twist stretch.

Chest Stretch

This exercise is used to stretch out the chest and the front of the shoulders; these muscles are particularly prone to tightening up, and should be closely monitored.

TECHNIQUE:
- Using a door frame, goal post, wall or any other appropriate object, raise your arm(s) to shoulder level with the elbows bent.
- Walk into the object, keeping the body facing directly forwards and preventing it from twisting. You should now feel the stretch across the chest and shoulders.

COMMON MISTAKES:
- Being too aggressive with the stretch and straining the shoulder muscles.
- Losing the neutral spine during the exercise.

Chest stretch.

ALTERNATIVES:
- Arm extension stretch.

Back Twist

This movement loosens up the body's rotator muscles, and mobilizes the spine.

TECHNIQUE:
- With one arm bent to 90 degrees at the elbow and out to the side, cross your leg over in the opposite direction.
- Use the opposite arm to aid the stretch.

COMMON MISTAKES:
- Allowing the arm and shoulder to come off the ground.

ALTERNATIVES:
- Seated and standing back twist.

Reverse Press-Up

The exercise is used to stretch the stomach muscles and mobilize the spine.

TECHNIQUE:
- Lying on your stomach, push upwards while keeping the hips on the ground.
- Hold for 5sec, then return to the floor and repeat the exercise.
- Push up only until the hips begin to leave the ground.
- Repeat five times.

COMMON MISTAKES:
- Being too aggressive with the stretch.
- Allowing the hips to leave the floor.

ALTERNATIVES:
- Back extension over a ball.

Back twist.

Reverse press-up.

Knees to Chest Stretch

A good stretch to loosen up the back and ensure the spine can flex freely.

TECHNIQUE:
- Lying on your back, pull your knees into your chest.

COMMON MISTAKE:
- Twisting your body as you stretch, because one side is tighter than the other.

ALTERNATIVES:
- Rounded back squat stretch, rounded back hamstring stretches.

Buttock Stretch

This stretch works the often tight deep rotator muscles within the hip.

TECHNIQUE:
- Lying on your back, cross one leg over the other.
- Push your knee away from you to feel a stretch in your buttocks.
- If necessary, increase the stretch by pulling the leg upwards and towards your chest.

COMMON MISTAKE:
- Holding the leg in the wrong place.
- Allowing the body to twist while stretching.

Knees to chest stretch.

Buttock stretch.

ALTERNATIVE:

- Seated leg across chest stretch.

Split-Leg Hamstring Stretch

A stretch for the hamstrings and adductor (groin) muscles.

TECHNIQUE:

- Sitting on the ground with your legs straight, spread your legs as wide as possible.
- Lean forwards to the middle so that you feel a stretch . . .
- . . . then lean down towards one foot.
- Repeat to the other side.
- Try to be aware of your toe position during these exercises. Vary them from facing upwards to pointing forwards and pointing backwards.

COMMON MISTAKES:

- Allowing the legs to bend when leaning forwards to stretch.
- Allowing the toes only to face in one direction e.g. away from the body, to compensate for tight hamstring muscles.

ALTERNATIVES:

- Seated and standing one-legged hamstring stretches, waiter's bow stretch.

Hip Flexor Stretch on an Object

Designed to stretch both the quadriceps muscle, and those that go over the front of the hip joint.

TECHNIQUE:

- With one foot flat on the floor and the other leg bent resting on an object – this could be a chair, goal post, Swiss ball or suchlike . . .
- . . . push the hips and position the body in a neutral spinal alignment.

Split-leg hamstring stretch.

COMMON MISTAKE:
- Allowing the hips or upper body to twist or bend.

ALTERNATIVE:
- Hip flexor stretch without an object, either kneeling or standing.

Calf Stretch

Used for stretching both the larger calf muscle higher up on the lower leg and the smaller soleus muscle below this. A tight soleus often inhibits ideal squatting technique.

TECHNIQUE:
- With a straight leg, let the rear foot drop towards the floor.
- Repeat this with a bent leg.
- Repeat with the other leg.

COMMON MISTAKE:
- Allowing the heel to leave the floor.

ALTERNATIVE:
- Standing calf stretch on a bench or step.

Hip flexor stretch on an object.

Calf stretch.

89

CHAPTER 4
Testing

The ultimate success of a conditioning programme is increased on-field performance. This is a subjective area, with many factors other than just fitness contributing to successful rugby. Therefore a variety of fitness tests are used to give an objective measure of the conditioning programme.

So why test? Testing is an important procedure as it gives information about how you are responding to the exercise programme. The results can be used as a powerful motivational tool, showing you the rewards of your efforts and highlighting any areas that need extra attention.

Bear in mind the law of diminishing returns: this hypothesis states that the more well trained the athlete, the smaller the expected gains that can made from training. Thus it is common to see large improvements when a conditioning programme is undertaken for the first time, however further development in subsequent phases may not be so dramatic. This fact should be included when evaluating your test results.

Consistency is important, and the testing situation and procedures need to be as similar as possible each time measurements are taken. This will ensure that any changes in results are from fitness alterations, and not from the testing procedure itself. Consistency can be maximized in the following ways:

- Performing the tests only when you are 100 per cent fit and free from injury or fatigue.

- Where applicable, by using the same person to test you.
- By ensuring the weather conditions are the same; for example wind direction, pitch conditions and so on.
- By performing the tests in the same order, and ideally at the same time of the day.
- By ensuring you use the same warm-up routine before the tests.

A large variety of tests can be used to monitor a training programme; the following represent the easiest that can be performed with the minimum of equipment. There is at least one test for each of the six training methods, as well as tests to monitor body composition.

TESTING BODY COMPOSITION

These tests allow you to gauge how your body changes over the time of your training programme.

Weight

Your bodyweight is a good guide as to how your body is changing when it is used in conjunction with body fat data.

REQUIREMENTS: Scales.

METHOD:
- Ensure the counter is adjusted to zero before standing on the scales.

CONSISTENCY:
- Use the same scales and clothing.
- Take the measurement at the same time of the day.

Test for Percentage Body Fat

The test reveals how much of your bodyweight is from stored fat.

REQUIREMENTS:
- Callipers.
- Trained tester for skinfold measurements (ask at your local fitness facility).

METHOD:
- The tester marks out certain sites on the body.
- Measurements are taken using skin callipers, and the total measurements are referenced against standard data to give a percentage body fat.

CONSISTENCY:
- Use same measurement sites.
- Use the same tester.

STRETCH TESTS

The stretch tests are used to analyse your flexibility, and each is designed so you either pass or fail. If a test is failed, then the suggested stretches should be followed until a pass can be achieved.

It is also important to repeat these tests regularly, as flexibility can change from day to day as stiffness arises from training and playing.

Overhead Squat

The overhead squat tests the flexibility of your calves, hamstrings, chest and shoulders. It also examines your spine's ability to go into extension.

REQUIREMENTS: A pole or towel.

METHOD:
- With your arms straight out above your head . . .
- . . . squat down to a 90-degree leg angle.

PASS:
- If in the 90-degree leg position your heels are on the floor, with a straight back and arms directly above the head.

FAIL:
- If your heels come off the floor.
- If your back rounds.
- If you cannot get your arms directly above the head.

Focus on calf stretch, hamstring stretch, hip stretch, reverse press-up and chest stretch.

CONSISTENCY:
- Use the same footwear.

Overhead squat test.

91

Back Twist Test

The test looks into the ability of your spine and the surrounding muscles to rotate.

REQUIREMENTS: N/a.

METHOD:
- With one arm bent to 90 degrees at the elbow and out to the side, cross your leg over in the opposite direction.
- Use the opposite arm to aid the stretch.
- Repeat to the other side.

PASS:
- If you can reach the leg to the opposite side without the arm coming off the floor.

FAIL:
- If you cannot get your leg to the other side without the arm coming off the floor.
- If you are not equal from side to side.

Focus on back twist stretch, chest stretch, and hip stretch.

CONSISTENCY: N/a.

Hip Flexor Test

The length of your thigh and front hip muscles are tested.

REQUIREMENTS: A bench.

METHOD:
- Sit on the edge of a bench and pull one leg into your chest.
- Roll backwards on to the bench while holding the leg in this position.
- Note the distance between the thigh and the bench, and how much the leg is bent.

PASS:
- If your thigh touches the bench with a 90-degree bend at the knee.

FAIL:
- If your thigh does not touch the bench, or if the leg is not bent to a 90-degree angle.
- If you have differences in flexibility from side to side.

Focus on hip flexor stretch.

Back twist test.

Hip flexor test.

CONSISTENCY:
• Ensure you wear the same clothing.

Knees to Chest Stretch Test

The test examines the spine's ability to go into flexion.

REQUIREMENTS: N/a

METHOD:
• Lying on your back, bring your knees up towards your chest.

PASS:
• If you can bring your knees all the way into your chest without the lower back feeling tight or the body twisting to one side.

FAIL:
• If you cannot get your knees to the chest without feeling a stretch in the back.

• If your body twists to one side while doing the stretch.

Focus on knee-to-chest stretch and split hamstring stretch.

CONSISTENCY: N/a.

Stretch Comparison Test

Perform all the set out stretches. Check for differences from side to side, for example left hamstring to right hamstring. Any large differences should be noted, and effort should be made to balance the sides out.

Stretch Tightness Tests

Perform all the stretches to check for tightness. If any muscles feel particularly tight,

Knees to chest stretch test.

perform stretches on that muscle until it loosens up and no longer feels stiff. These test are important, as stiffness can arise suddenly in muscles, and from many different causes.

PLYOMETRIC TESTS

Vertical Jump

This test is an indicator of your fast-speed strength.

REQUIREMENTS:
- Measuring tape.
- Pen or chalk.
- A wall.

METHOD:
- With a pen or chalk, reach upwards as high as possible with your right arm and make a mark on the wall.
- With a slight counter movement (dip downwards), jump as high as possible and

make a mark with your pen at the highest point of the jump.

The vertical jump height is the difference between your standing still mark and highest mark made while jumping.

CONSISTENCY:
- Use the same footwear.
- Perform at the same wall.
- Ensure you reach as high as possible when making the initial standing measurement.
- Ensure the mark is made at the highest point of your jump.

TESTS FOR AGILITY

The T-test shows your ability to stop, start and change direction.

The T- Test

REQUIREMENTS:
- Four equal-sized markers, for example cones, rugby balls . . .

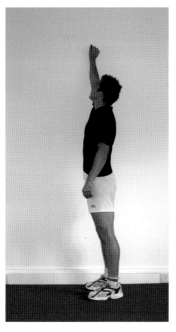  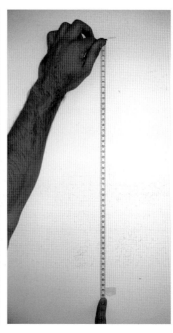

Vertical jump test.

- Measuring tape.
- Tester.
- Stopwatch.

METHOD:
- With the course arranged as below . . .
- . . . run 10m forwards and touch marker B with your left hand.
- Using lateral movement, touch marker C with your right hand.
- Using lateral movement, go 10m to the left, touching marker D with your left hand.
- Laterally move back to marker B, touching it with your right hand.
- Go 10m back through the start line using back pedal.
- Start the stopwatch on the initial movement, and stop it when the finish line is broken.

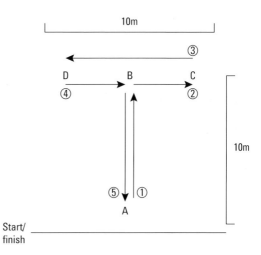

The schematic of the T-test agility drill.

CONSISTENCY:
- Use the same-sized markers.
- Use the same tester, and ensure that each marker is touched.

TESTS FOR STRENGTH

These strength tests give an indication of your ability to produce slow-speed maximum strength.

Three Repetition Lift

REQUIREMENTS:
- A spotter.
- Equipment for bench press, bent over row and squat (leg press or deadlift if squat unavailable).

Please note that *no other* exercises should be used, *for safety reasons*.

METHOD:
- Perform a few warm-up sets, using a gradually heavier but comfortable weight.
- Select a weight that you estimate could be lifted three times.
- Perform three reps, keeping the correct technique throughout.
- After 3–5min rest, repeat, using a heavier/lighter weight, depending on how the last lifting attempt felt; for instance, if you performed only two reps, reduce the weight, and if you achieved three reps, increase it.
- Repeat until you find your true three repetitions maximum load.

CONSISTENCY:
- Use the same-sized weights: for example, the circumference of the weight plate.
- Ensure your technique is correct for all repetitions.
- Take the same rest periods, and use the same exercise order.

SPRINTING TESTS

The sprint tests measure your acceleration (40m test), your maximum speed and speed

endurance (100m test), and your anaerobic power (400m sprint test.)

40m and 100m

REQUIREMENTS:
- Stopwatch.
- Tester.
- Athletics track or length of a rugby field.

METHOD:
- Mark out a distance of 40m or 100m.
- On your first movement the tester starts the stopwatch.
- Run the required distance.
- The tester stops the clock the moment your chest breaks the finish line.

CONSISTENCY:
- Use the same footwear.
- Ensure the pitch and weather conditions are the same.
- Use the same starting technique, for example crouching, standing . . .
- Keep the measured distance constant.

400m (or one lap)

REQUIREMENTS:
- Stopwatch.
- Athletics track or perimeter of rugby pitch.
- Tester (optional).

METHOD:
- On your first movement start the watch.
- Complete one lap of the athletics track or rugby pitch.
- Stop the clock the moment your chest breaks the finish line.

CONSISTENCY:
- Ensure the pitch and weather conditions are the same.
- Ensure the distance is kept constant.

AEROBIC ENDURANCE TESTS

This test shows your aerobic capacity and ability to tolerate lactic acid.

Six-Minute Run Test

REQUIREMENTS:
- Athletics track or perimeter of a pitch.
- Stopwatch.

METHOD:
- Run as many laps as possible during the 6min.
- Record the distance as accurately as possible; for example, 5 laps and 40m.

CONSISTENCY:
- Ensure that the weather and pitch conditions are the same.

Testing Order

The described tests should be performed on the same day. To ensure fatigue does not affect the results of the tests, use the order and minimum recovery times as set out below.

Through following this test order and recovery times it is possible to record accurately the data about yourself and your physical abilities. This allows your progression over time to be charted.

Obtaining Test Data

It may not be possible to record all the test data at every suggested testing period – for instance, perhaps there is no partner available, or some such problem. It can also be found that the testing conditions are not the same, for example pitch conditions are firmer in

TABLE 2: IDEAL TEST ORDER AND RECOVERY TIMES

Test order	Type of test	Individual test	Rest between individual tests	Rest between types of test
1st	Body composition	Weight	–	–
Warm-up: Perform 5 minutes light jogging followed by the sprint drills				
2nd	Flexibility	Stretch test	–	0 minutes
3rd	Plyometric	Vertical jump	–	0 minutes
4th	Agility	T-Test	–	5 minutes
		Bench press	5 minutes	–
5th	Strength	Bent over row	5 minutes	–
		Squat	–	5 minutes
		40m	5 minutes	–
6th	Anaerobic	100m	10 minutes	–
		400m	–	45 minutes
7th	Aerobic	6 minute run	–	–

the summer as compared to winter. These inaccuracies should be noted down so they can be included in the evaluation of scores. Nevertheless, any test data is better than none, and efforts should be made to get as much data as possible at the prescribed test times.

Interpreting Scores

The initial tests provide you with a benchmark at the beginning of the training programme; subsequent testing will show the effects of the training programme. It is expected that there will be improvements in all test data at the end of the off season as compared to the beginning. During the playing season it may be harder to make advances in fitness due to the demands of playing matches – in fact it is not uncommon to see slight decreases in physical performance. This is a consequence of the long blocks of competitive games, which impedes training.

Any individual scores that have not changed as greatly as, or have decreased more than, the other physical attributes, need examining. The following questions should be asked:

Was the testing procedure consistent with the last set of measurements taken?
Think of any possible inconsistencies that may have affected the data, such as a waterlogged pitch, wind direction, or suchlike.

Has an injury affected the training method or testing procedure?
Injuries can greatly interfere with training; for instance, a wrist injury may have prevented you from doing any bench press over the last few weeks.

Am I already strong in this training method as compared to the others?
For example, you have just finished training for the cross-country season (aerobic training), but have never lifted weights before (resistance training).

Has the training method been given equal attention compared to the others?
You may have performed every strength training session, but only half the prescribed number of aerobic sessions.

These questions reveal the reasons behind the situation where one score changes differently in comparison to the others. Answering 'yes' to questions one and two suggests that you should not be too concerned about the test score, as the procedure and/or programme has not been consistent. A 'yes' to question three shows how the 'law of diminishing returns' affects your results. It is important not to be discouraged by this. Question four reveals which training method you are having the most difficulty fitting into your weekly schedule, and the reasons why you are missing these sessions need to be examined and a plan to counteract this problem implemented.

The above tests give a large amount of data about your physical abilities and should be recorded in the results table found on p. 177 in the Appendix.

CHAPTER 5
The Principles of Programme Design

The structure and design of a fitness training programme is a scientific process following certain principles and rules. The theory of periodization is the exercise theory that incorporates such rules and governs how a training programme is structured and organized. The concept incorporates all aspects of fitness to ensure the athlete continues to improve from year to year without suffering from overtraining or injury.

Periodization has become the underlying theory and basis for all élite athletes' training programmes. However, its widespread popularity and proven success at the highest level has yet to permeate down to the amateur ranks. In this chapter the basic fundamental principles are described and summarized. (For a comprehensive and more in-depth discussion on periodization, *see* Further Reading, *The Theory and Methodology of Training*, Tudor O. Bompa 1998, or the other sources referenced[3, 13, 14] therein.)

Periodization divides the year into differing lengths of time, from the whole year down to individual weeks and training sessions. Individual weeks are grouped together and comprise a specific training protocol. It is through the combination of the different training protocols that the body continues to improve in physical performance without experiencing overtraining or undue injury. The types of training used are influenced by the rules of how to manipulate the training variables of intensity, volume and specificity. These are discussed after examining how the training year is divided.

DIVISION OF THE TRAINING YEAR

The training year can be divided into successively smaller blocks of time. First, the calendar year can be divided into two types of season: the in-season and off-season. The in-season covers the time from the first to last competitive game of the sports season. The off-season is the time between the last competitive match of the previous season to the first game of the next season. Most sports have just one in-season – rugby, soccer, cricket – but some have more: for example, netball has a winter and a summer league, and therefore has two in-seasons and two off-seasons (*see* Tables 3 and 4).

The objective of the off-season is to increase the player's physical abilities for the next in-season; this will result in improved on-field performances. That of the in-season is to maintain, or increase where possible, the physical abilities of the player while ensuring he is able to perform at his highest level for competitive matches. The bulk of the training focuses on maintaining current levels while allowing time to achieve peak performance in the games played. When gaps appear in the fixture calendar, attempts are made to increase fitness levels.

TABLE 3: THE TYPICAL SEASON STRUCTURE FOR RUGBY UNION

Jan	Feb	Mar	Apr	May	Jun	Jul	Aug	Sept	Oct	Nov	Dec
In-season				Off-season				In-season			

TABLE 4: THE TYPICAL SEASON STRUCTURE FOR NETBALL

Jan	Feb	Mar	Apr	May	Jun	Jul	Aug	Sept	Oct	Nov	Dec
In-season		Off-season		In-season			Off-season		In-season		

The two types of season are further divided by grouping separate weeks together into blocks of time. Within these blocks a certain type of training is used to achieve a training objective: for example, building a fitness base, maintaining current levels, rest and recovery. These goals are achieved by using different exercises and manipulating the training variables. The in-season and off-season are arranged differently to allow their individual purposes to be achieved.

Division of the Off-Season

Initially the off-season is used to recover from the stresses of the previous in-season. The training then focuses on increasing fitness levels for the next. To maximize fitness, a logical progression is followed that successively builds up a player's levels of conditioning.

The fitness levels are developed optimally through first creating a fitness base, then gradually increasing the training to mimic the playing demands of actual games. To accomplish these goals the off-season is divided into five training blocks (*see* Table 5).

The recovery block at the beginning of the off-season gives the athlete time to recharge both physically and mentally before training begins in preparation for the next in-season. This block has no prescribed training for the player to follow, with the emphasis on relaxation and keeping active through other activities, such as squash, or a game of soccer.

The base fitness training block is used to develop general conditioning themes that underlie all exercises and good health; for example, aerobic power to sustain activities, correcting muscle-length imbalances, increasing muscle strength all over the body.

The general fitness training block employs and develops techniques and attributes which must be present to receive the maximum benefits from the more specific training routines that follow; for example, through increasing muscle size, higher levels of maximum strength can be attained.

TABLE 5: DIVISION OF THE OFF-SEASON INTO FIVE TRAINING BLOCKS

Off-season

Recovery	Base fitness training	General fitness training	Sport specific training	Position specific training

TABLE 6: DIVISION OF THE OFF-SEASON INTO BLOCKS INCORPORATING RECOVERY WEEKS

Off-season

Recovery	Base fitness training	General fitness training	Recovery	Sport specific training	Position specific training	Recovery

The sport-specific block concentrates on the demands of the sport played, and the training focuses on developing the physical attributes that directly influence playing performance.

The position-specific block is tailored to replicate and develop the actual qualities that are stressed during competitive matches. The block brings the physical attributes of the athlete to new heights in preparation for the beginning of the next in-season. Different positions use an exercise protocol that replicates their required roles for successful on-field performance.

Recovery blocks are also placed in addition to the initial block during the off-season. This gives a period of relief from the training stresses to free the body from fatigue. The weeks are planned in advance (*see* Table 6), but can be implemented whenever the athlete is feeling too tired to effectively perform the training routines. The block follows a prescribed training protocol (unlike the recovery block at the beginning of off-season), but it is performed with a great reduction in overall stress. It usually lasts for one to two weeks.

How long each block lasts varies from sport to sport, being influenced by the length of the off-season, specific fitness goals, and player requirements. In general, each block usually lasts between one to four weeks, though this can vary greatly.

Within the five blocks, different training protocols are applied to provide successively more challenging stimuli, thereby maximizing fitness increases by the start of the next in-season.

Division of the In-Season

The in-season has three blocks: maintenance, recovery and development. Which block is used depends upon whether the athlete is involved in a competitive game during that week (*see* Table 7).

The maintenance block focuses on keeping all the physical attributes at their current standards. The amount of training is kept to a minimum, but at a level that ensures the athlete does not suffer from detraining. The maintenance block can last for long periods of time – twenty weeks plus – dependent upon the fixture calendar.

The development block is placed at times where there are no scheduled games. The body can be subjected to a greater training stress as it does not need to be fresh for a match, therefore training volume is increased as the athlete develops his physical abilities. The development block can last from one week to three to four weeks plus, depending on the fixture list, cancelled fixtures or non-selection.

The recovery blocks serve the same role as that during the off-season. It allows the body a chance to recover from previous training and competitive stresses.

The training blocks can be further broken down into the individual weeks that they comprise. The weeks within a training block use similar training routines but with subtle changes: for instance, more repetitions, less rest and so on, as opposed to different exercises. These changes within a block ensure that the body's fitness levels are progressed optimally.

The Training Week

The individual weeks contain training sessions, and these are divided to cover one or more of the different training methods, such as sprint, agility, strength training. The different training methods are grouped together according to how they affect each other; for instance, aerobic training and strength training can diminish each other's effect if they are performed in the same session.

The number of training sessions performed each week is dictated by the time of the year, the desired outcome, and personal time and preference. Thus a full-time athlete will be able to devote more time to training than someone who has a nine-to-five office job. The number of sessions required to be done is not the same all year round, being influenced by the playing season and training goal; therefore during a recovery block, for example, very few training sessions are performed.

The training session itself is divided into a warm-up, the main session, and a cool-down. The warm-up and cool-down allow the body and mind to prepare and recover from the actual training that is performed during the main session.

TABLE 7: DIVISION OF THE IN-SEASON IN TRAINING BLOCKS

In-season

Maintenance	Rec	Maintenance	Dev	Maintenance	Dev

Key: Rec = Recovery block, Dev = Development block.

Exercise Protocols

The exercise protocol is the blueprint of what you actually do during an individual training session, and is perhaps the most important aspect of a periodized conditioning programme. Within each training method the various exercises, techniques and routines can be formed into thousands of different protocols, some of which will produce the desired result more effectively than others. Each training method has more than one protocol.

A protocol is designed so that it produces a certain training outcome; thus a slow-speed strength resistance-training protocol improves maximum strength, while a rugby-specific movement agility protocol is designed to fine tune and prepare the player's agility skills for competition.

The training protocols are aligned with training blocks, so that a certain type of training is used during a specific type of training block; for example, the base fitness block uses a steady pace and 300m protocol for aerobic and sprint methods. The manipulation of the training variables as governed by periodization decides which training protocol to align with which block.

SUMMARY OF THE TRAINING YEAR

It can be seen that the calendar year is divided into two types of season, comprising different

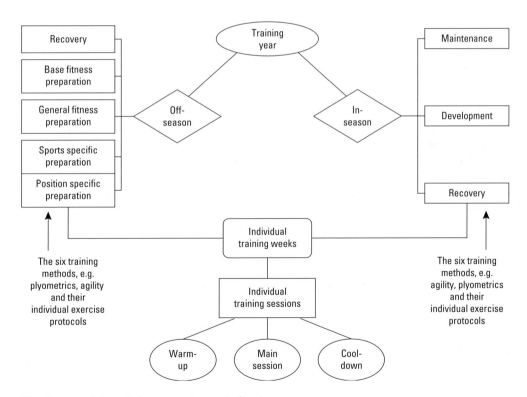

The division of the training year using periodization.

103

training blocks, each of which uses a certain type of exercise protocol. The training blocks comprise the individual weeks, which at the basic level are comprised of training sessions.

MANIPULATING THE TRAINING VARIABLES

The order of the training blocks, and the subtle variations within them over each week, are designed according to periodization's manipulation of the training variables. The training performed is organized according to three training variables:

- *Intensity* – the relative performance compared to the athlete's maximum ability.
- *Volume* – the amount of exercise performed.
- *Specificity* – how closely the exercise replicates on-field requirements.

The theory of periodization works by altering the three variables throughout the year. Many different methods have been proposed as to how to alter these to produce optimal adaptation from training and thereby maximize performance, and each model is supported by research into its relative merits and disadvantages. Even so, it is easy to feel swamped by the conflicting information, and to become confused as to how to apply peri-

odization to your training programme. However, this process need not be daunting, and the following sections describe how it can be easily achieved.

Performance

The ultimate goal of periodization, and the process of varying the intensity, volume and specificity of training, is to increase fitness levels and positively influence performance to the greatest extent.

The performance levels are increased during the off-season so that the following in-season begins with the player capable of higher levels.

Intensity

Intensity is defined as the level of exercise in comparison to the athlete's maximum performance; for example, for resistance training it is the weight lifted in comparison to the heaviest possible weight one can lift (one repetition maximum); running is viewed in comparison to maximum running speed. The relationship between pain and intensity should be noted. A 100m sprint is of very high intensity, running close to maximum speed. A three-mile jog is performed at a lower intensity, running at a considerably slower speed in comparison to the 100m sprint. However, the three-mile run will produce far more discomfort and pain than the 100m sprint.

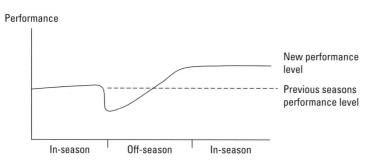

The effect on performance from manipulating the training variables. (Earlier versions of this can be found by M.H. Stone.)[4, 10]

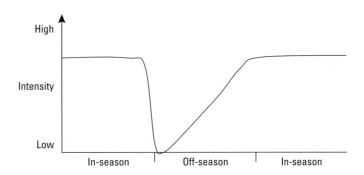

The manipulation of intensity during the training year. (Earlier versions of this can be found by M.H. Stone et al.)[15, 16]

Intensity is varied during the course of the calendar year to produce an optimal training adaptation.

The intensity levels are kept high during the in-season, while during the off-season the intensity starts low and gradually increases. It is altered by using a protocol that changes the speed of the drill, the force encountered, or the weight lifted.

Volume

Volume refers to the amount of exercise performed. This can be expressed in a variety of ways depending upon the training method being used. In resistance training the volume can be defined by the number of sets performed, duration of exercise or the amount of weight lifted per session. Sprinting and jog-ging are expressed by distance covered, while agility and plyometrics are viewed in terms of repetitions or distance per exercise. The over-all volume of training for training methods is varied during the year.

Volume is kept low during the in-season to allow for team practices and to ensure the player is fresh for matches. The start of the off-season sees the highest volume of training. The volume is altered by changing the length of the drill or number of repetitions performed. The variation of volume is the opposite to that of intensity: when volume is high, intensity is low, and vice versa. This makes sense, as asking you to run twice the distance or perform twice the number of reps will mean you must perform it at a slower speed or use a lighter weight to complete the task successfully.

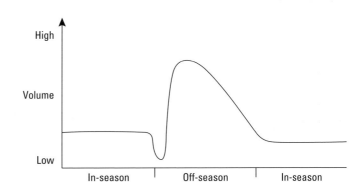

The manipulation of volume during the training year. (Earlier versions of this can be found by M.H. Stone et al.)[15, 16]

Specificity

Specificity refers to how much an exercise simulates the encountered environment of a match situation. This incorporates speed of movement, distance covered and movement patterns. A 30-minute jog is of low specificity because you would never perform this during a rugby match, while special endurance training is of high specificity because it closely replicates the movement patterns performed during competition, involving acceleration/deceleration and non-linear movements.

Specificity does not need to be high at all times of the year. Through performing less specific training, a fitness base is formed that allows higher performance levels to be reached when the training returns to more specific exercises. The pattern of variation is the same as for intensity, the athlete begins the off-season with low levels, and gradually increasing to their highest levels for the start of the in-season, where they remain throughout. Specificity is altered by changing the exercises performed.

Combining the Variables

The combination and interplay of these variables comprise the foundation upon which your training programme is built, and are the reason why it is structured the way it is. Together the three variables optimally enhance playing performance.

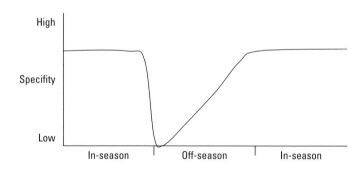

The manipulation of specificity during the training year.
(Earlier versions of this can be found by M.H. Stone, *et al.*)[15, 16]

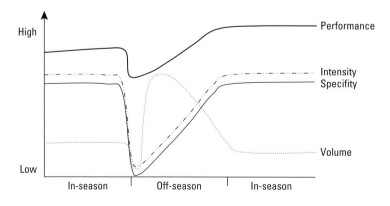

The manipulation of the training variables and the effect on performance. (Earlier versions of this can be found by M.H. Stone, *et al.*)[15, 16]

SUMMARY

Periodization covers two aspects: the division of the training year and manipulation of the three training variables.

The training year is divided into two seasons: the off-season (where no games occur) and the in-season (containing all the competitive matches). The off-season is divided into five blocks, while the in-season is divided into three.

Each block uses a different exercise protocol for the different training methods, for example aerobic endurance training, agility training, and so on. The blocks are made up from individual weeks, which slightly change the programme from one to the next. These individual weeks are comprised of the different training sessions, which are each compiled of a warm-up, a main session and a cool-down.

The manipulation of the three training variables sees the intensity, volume and specificity of the exercise stimulus altered during the course of the year. This is the most effective method to optimize training adaptations and avoid overtraining. The result is increased fitness from year to year.

CHAPTER 6

Designing a Training Programme for Rugby

To apply the principles of periodization to a rugby fitness programme the concepts discussed previously are used to shape the protocols within the six training methods. The different protocols contain all the training programmes for you to follow.

In this chapter each protocol within the six training methods is examined, along with the techniques used to progress them from week to week during a block. Before the protocols are examined, however, the year needs to be divided up in accordance with periodization theory.

THE YEARLY STRUCTURE

The typical rugby season runs from September to April. Applying the periodization groupings to this gives an in-/off-season structure as below.

TABLE 8: THE DIVISION OF THE YEAR INTO SEASONS

Jan	Feb	Mar	Apr	May	Jun	Jul	Aug	Sept	Oct	Nov	Dec
In-season				Off-season				In-season			

TABLE 9: THE DIVISION OF THE SEASONS INTO BLOCKS

Off-season

Recovery	Base fitness training	General fitness training	Sport-specific training	Position-specific training

In-season

Maintenance	Rec	Maintenance	Dev	Maintenance	Dev

Key: Rec = Recovery, Dev = Development.

Training Protocols

The six training methods are divided into individual training protocols. Each method varies in how many protocols it has. As explained, the protocols use a selection of exercises and techniques to alter the exercise stimulus and create the desired training effect. It is through aligning the protocols with different training blocks within each method that the variables of volume, intensity and specificity can be manipulated as is necessary to achieve peak performance.

The training protocols used within each block give the structure needed to alter intensity, volume and specificity. In addition to this, an element of the training programme is slightly altered each week; subtle changes are made to the rest periods, exercise volume and/or intensity, and these slight alterations ensure the body continues to respond to the exercise stimulus, and further allows the manipulation of the training variables.

Each training method is now examined, showing all the training protocols and the methods used for weekly progression.

AEROBIC ENDURANCE TRAINING

Aerobic endurance training is designed to increase the athlete's aerobic power and lactate tolerance.

The Aerobic Endurance Training Protocols

Aerobic endurance training uses six protocols to provide the different levels of volume, intensity and specificity needed throughout the year.

Steady Pace Protocol

The protocol has the athlete jogging at a constant pace for the duration of the session.

- Running type: Lap or straight line running.
- Reps: 1.
- Exercise duration: 20–30min.
- Exercise technique: A constant pace is maintained throughout (avoid accelerating towards the end of the run).

Intervals with Recovery Protocol

The protocol intersperses intervals of a quicker jogging with lower intensity jogging to allow recovery.

- Running type: Traditional, lap or line running.
- Duration: Work intervals 1–3min, recovery interval 1min.
- Intervals ratio: 3:1–1:1 (work: recovery)
- Reps: 5–10 work intervals.
- Technique: Using the interval ratio and rep number, intersperse fast jogging with slower speed recovery.

The aerobic endurance training protocols.

Intervals with Rest

This protocol uses periods of intense running interspersed by periods of rest – that is, complete cessation of activity.

- Running type: Lap, traditional, line running.
- Duration: Work interval 6min, rest interval 2–6min.
- Interval ratio: 3:1–1:1 (work: rest).
- Reps: 3 work intervals.
- Technique: 100 per cent effort for the work interval, then complete cessation of activity while resting, e.g. very gentle walking or standing still.

Special Endurance

This protocol is designed to mimic the demands of a game. The protocol uses a variety of speeds and movement types over an 80/100m course, dependent on position.

- Running type: Line running.
- Duration: 80/100m course.
- Reps: 20–40.
- Technique: As per course layout.

Maintenance

Used to maintain the aerobic power and lactate tolerance levels at their current standards.

- Running type: Line running.
- Duration: 80/100m course.
- Reps: 20.
- Technique: As per course layout.

Recovery Protocol

Uses a short, light run to aid the body's recovery processes.

- Running type: Lap or traditional running
- Reps: 1
- Duration: 15min
- Technique: Comfortable easy pace

Progressing the Aerobic Endurance Protocols

These protocols can be altered slightly week by week during the training block to maximize the body's response to the exercise stimulus.

Steady Pace

The protocol is progressed weekly through increasing the duration of the running. The jogging is gradually increased by five minutes each week until thirty minutes can be performed. Once this is achieved the duration of the jog is kept constant, but the speed at which the running is performed can be increased.

Week 1:   20min
Week 2:   25min
Week 3+: 30min

Intervals with Recovery

Progression is achieved by altering the work-to-rest ratio of the intervals during the first three weeks. In any subsequent weeks thereafter the speed of each interval is increased, with the work-to-rest ratios remaining the same as that performed in week three. The changing of the work : recovery ratio alters both the intensity and volume of the sessions.

Week 1:   3min: 1min × 5
Week 2:   2min: 1min × 7
Week 3+: 1min: 1min × 10
Key: 3min higher intensity: 1min lower intensity × 5 reps of high intensity

Intervals with Rest

The protocol is made more challenging through progression of the work-to-rest ratio for the first three weeks. This uses a gradual increase of the rest period between intervals, therefore allowing a higher intensity to be performed in each run. In any subsequent weeks after the first three, the speed of each interval is increased, with the work-to-rest ratios remaining the same.

Week 1:   6min: 2min × 3
Week 2:   6min: 4min × 3
Week 3+: 6min: 6min × 3
Key: 6min higher intensity: 6min
           rest × 3 reps of high intensity

Special Endurance

The athlete is progressively challenged week by week through increases in the number of repetitions performed. In any subsequent weeks the player can increase the demand by increasing the quality of each repetition.

Week 1:   80/100m special endurance
           run × 20
Week 2:   80/100m special endurance
           run × 30
Week 3+: 80/100m special endurance
           run × 40

Maintenance Protocol

The objective of this protocol is to keep the athlete's aerobic fitness levels at their current standard. This can be achieved without needing to vary the protocol from week to week. Therefore the training remains the same throughout the protocol.

Recovery Protocol

The recovery protocol is designed to help the nervous system free itself from fatigue. To do this the light jog does not need to be advanced, therefore the training protocol remains the same throughout.

SPRINT TRAINING

The sprint training methodology is designed to increase acceleration, maximum speed and speed endurance.

Sprint Training Protocols

There are six individual protocols used during the sprint training methodology. They each use a selection of sprinting distances to achieve the training methods' objectives. The protocols are classified according to the distances run or the outcome they intend to produce.

The sprint training protocols.

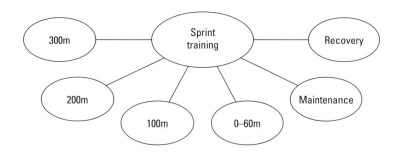

The 300m Sprint

Using 300m sprints, the protocol heavily taxes the anaerobic medium energy system and therefore enhances anaerobic power, lactate tolerance and speed endurance.

- Distance: 300m.
- Reps: 4.
- Rest: 3–9min.
- Technique: Running at a constant pace throughout. The athlete should aim to run on the balls of the feet for the duration of the sprint.

The 200m Sprint

The 200m protocol requires a significant contribution from the medium anaerobic system, which positively influences lactate tolerance, anaerobic power and speed endurance.

- Distance: 200m.
- Reps: 4.
- Rest: 3–9min.
- Technique: Running at a constant pace on the balls of the feet.

The 100m Sprint

The 100m distance emphasizes the fast anaerobic energy system while enhancing neuro-muscular co-ordination. The protocol increases the player's speed endurance, maximum speed and acceleration.

- Distance: 100m.
- Reps: 4.
- Rest: 3–9min.
- Technique: Focus on explosive acceleration using the arms and staying on the balls of the feet.

The 0–60m Sprint

The protocol uses shorter, game-specific distances to prepare the athlete for competition, developing acceleration and maximum speed. The Forwards and Backs have slightly different routines to reflect the different requirements of their relative positions.

- Distances: Backs: 60, 60, 40, 30, 20. Forwards: 60, 40, 30, 20, 20.
- Reps: 1 of each.
- Rest: 2–6min.
- Technique: Focus on explosive acceleration using the arms and staying on the balls of the feet.

Maintenance

The protocol uses a variety of distances to stress the different aspects of sprinting, and maintain them at their current levels.

- Distances: 20m, 40m, 60m, 100m, 250m.
- Reps: 1 × each distance.
- Rest: 5min between reps.
- Technique: As per individual protocols above.

Recovery

This training employs some easy-paced sprints to assist the central nervous system during the recovery process.

- Distance: 100m.
- Reps: 10.
- Rest: 30sec.
- Technique: Running at an easy pace at equivalent to 60 per cent of maximum speed, e.g. if you run 100m in 12sec, then perform the repetitions in 17sec. This feels very slow, but aids in the body's recovery mechanisms.

Progressing the Sprint Training Protocols

The protocols are all progressed through increasing the rest periods from week to week. This allows higher intensities to be used during the protocol – for example, a higher speed can be attained during each repetition as more recovery time is available.

The 300m, 200m and 100m Sprints

The rest period is increased from 3min rest in the first week to 9min rest in the third week. Any further weeks uses the same rest periods as in the third week.

Week 1:   4 × 300m/200m/100m with
          3min rest
Week 2:   4 × 300m/200m/100m with
          6min rest
Week 3+: 4 × 300m/200m/100m with
          9min rest

The 0–60m Sprint

This protocol is progressed as above, but with the rest periods being increased from 2min through to 6min in the third week of the protocol.

Week 1:   1 × 60, 60, 40, 30, 20 with
          2min rest
Week 2:   1 × 60, 60, 40, 30, 20 with
          4min rest

Week 3+: 1 × 60, 60, 40, 30, 20 with
          6min rest

Maintenance

The objective of this protocol is to maintain the acceleration, maximum speed and speed endurance levels at their current standard. This is achieved by performing the selection of distances as described previously. It is therefore unnecessary to vary the training from week to week.

Recovery Protocol

The purpose of the protocol is to help the nervous system's recovery, and this is achieved through the easy-paced sprints. Therefore the training protocol remains the same throughout.

AGILITY TRAINING

Agility training increases a player's ability to change his speed, direction and type of movement.

Agility Training Protocol

The training protocols are distinguished by the exercises they use, which vary from simple movements to complex drills that mimic the demands of Rugby Union. The training method is split into five protocols.

The agility training protocols.

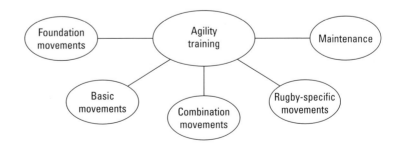

Foundation Movements Protocol

The drills are designed to develop the basic movement patterns that underlie all multidirectional and agility movements.

- Exercises: Lateral running, back pedal, forward and backward diagonal running.
- Reps: 2/exercise/direction: e.g. 2 lateral runs to the right, and 2 lateral runs to the left.
- Distance: 10–20m.
- Rest: 1min between reps.
- Technique: Use explosive movements without compromising technique.

Basic Movements Protocol

The drills are designed to reinforce basic movement patterns and teach simple transitions between movement types.

- Exercises: Weaving runs, turn and run shuttles, forward and backward zigzag runs.
- Reps: 2/exercise/direction.
- Distance: 20–30m.
- Rest: 1min between reps.
- Technique: Use explosive movements without compromising technique.

Combination Movements Protocol

The drills develop the ability to change between movement types.

- Exercises: Square drill, diamond drill, forward-facing Z-pattern runs, lateral weaving runs.
- Reps: 2/exercise.
- Distance: 5–10m for square and diamond drills, 25–45m for Z-pattern runs.
- Rest: 1min between reps.

- Technique: Use explosive movements without compromising technique.

Rugby-Specific Movement Protocol

The exercises develop to change between movement types, while including some rugby-specific elements.

- Exercises: Sideways facing Z-pattern run, forward Z-pattern run with side step, zigzag running with side step, the cross-agility drill.
- Reps: 2/exercise.
- Distance: 25–45m for Z-pattern and zigzag run, 10–20m for turn and sprint shuttles and cross-agility drill.
- Rest: 1min between reps.
- Technique: Ensure you use realistic rugby side steps.

Maintenance

The protocol focuses on maintaining the agility skills at their current levels.

- Exercises: Forward Z-pattern run with side step, sideways-facing Z-pattern run, zigzag run with side step, cross-agility drill, diamond drill and square drill.
- Reps: 1/exercise.
- Distance: 25m and 10m for rugby-specific movement exercises. 5m and 25m for combination movement exercises.
- Rest: 1min between reps.
- Technique: As per the individual exercises.

Progression of the Agility Training Protocol

The progression within the agility training protocols is implemented by increasing the length of the exercises.

Foundation Movement Protocol

The exercises are progressed from 10m per exercise up to 20m per exercise in Week 3. This represents the maximum length of the drill. In any subsequent weeks the distance is kept the same, and focus is placed on increasing the speed of the drill without losing correct technique.

Week 1:   10m/exercise
Week 2:   15m/exercise
Week 3+: 20m/exercise

Basic Movement Protocol

These drills are progressed exactly as for the foundation movements except the distances are increased from 20m through to 30m per exercise in Week 3. The exercise remains at that length for any subsequent weeks, as continually extending the length may hinder the quality of the movement.

Week 1:   20m/exercise
Week 2:   25m/exercise
Week 3+: 30m/exercise

Combination Movement Protocol

The exercises are again increased in length each week. The two types of exercise require increases from 5m to 10m and 25m to 45m respectively. The lengths of the exercises in Week 3 are the longest that they should be taken to.

Week 1:   5m and 25m/exercise
Week 2:   7.5m and 35m/exercise
Week 3+: 10m and 45m /exercise

Rugby-Specific Movement Protocol

These exercises are increased in length depending upon the type of exercise. Week 3 represents the longest length the exercises are performed at, with all subsequent weeks emphasizing increased speed of the movement.

Week 1:   25m and 10m/exercise
Week 2:   30m and 15m/exercise
Week 3+: 30m and 20m/exercise

Maintenance

The aim of maintenance protocol is to keep the player's agility skills at their current standard. This is achieved through simply performing the exercises without the need to change the stimulus week to week.

PLYOMETRIC TRAINING

The aim of plyometric training is to develop the stretch-shortening cycle and improve the

The plyometric training protocols.

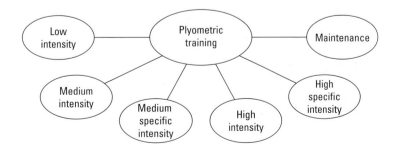

energy contribution it provides to fast-speed strength movements.

Plyometric Training Protocol

The protocols are classified according to the intensity of the exercises and how closely they replicate on-field demands. There are six protocols used within this training method.

Low Intensity

The exercises all use two-footed landings and take-offs.

- Exercises: Squat jump, standing long jump, diagonal jumps, lateral jumps.
- Sets: 2/exercise.
- Reps: 8–12.
- Rest: 90sec between sets.
- Technique: As per the individual exercises.

Medium Intensity

The exercises are based on two-footed jumps, but are performed in a series of multiple jumps.

- Exercises: Split-squat jump, double-leg hop, double-leg zigzag hop, sideways hopping.
- Sets: 2/exercise.
- Reps: 8–12.
- Rest: 90sec.
- Technique: As per individual exercises.

Medium Specific Intensity

The medium specific exercises more closely replicate the on-field demands of rugby by introducing sprints at the end of each exercise. The plyometric part of the exercise is the same intensity to the previous protocol.

- Exercises: Cycled split squat with movement, double leg hop + 15m lateral sprint, double-leg zigzag hop +15m forward sprint, lateral cone jump + 15m turn and sprint.
- Sets: 2/exercise.
- Reps: 8–12.
- Rest: 90sec.
- Technique: As per individual exercises.

High Intensity

These exercises increase the demands placed on the body by using just one leg for landing and take-off. The protocol should only be performed if the previously set out criteria are met.

- Exercises: Single-leg squat jump, single-leg bound, single-leg zigzag hop, single-leg lateral jump.
- Sets: 2/exercise.
- Reps: 8–12 reps and 20–30m.
- Rest: 90sec between sets.
- Technique: As per individual exercises.

High Specific Intensity

Designed to more closely replicate the demands encountered during matches. The exercises are performed off one leg, but at the end of each drill a short sprint is performed.

- Exercises: Single-leg hop + 15m lateral sprint, double arm single leg bound, single-leg zigzag hop + 15m sprint, single-leg lateral jump + 15m turn and sprint.
- Sets: 2/exercise.
- Reps: 8–12 reps and 20m–30m.
- Rest: 90sec between sets.
- Technique: As per individual exercises.

Maintenance

The protocol is designed to keep the stretch-shortening cycle's abilities at their current standard. This is achieved by performing a selection of exercises from the previous protocols.

- Exercises: Medium-specific or high-specific exercises.
- Sets: 1/exercise.
- Reps: 8 reps or 20m/exercise.
- Rest: 90sec between sets.
- Technique: As per individual exercises.

Progression of the Plyometric Training Protocols

The protocols are advanced by increasing the volume of the exercises. This is achieved through changing the number of repetitions performed, or the length of the drill.

Low, Medium and Medium Specific Intensity Protocol

These protocols all change the number of repetitions performed each week. The number of reps per exercise is increased from eight in week one, to twelve in week three. This is the uppermost number of reps performed so that fatigue does not interfere with the quality of the exercises. In any subsequent weeks thereafter focus is placed on increasing the distance/height achieved during each repetition.

Week 1: 8 reps/exercise
Week 2: 10 reps/exercise
Week 3+: 12 reps/exercise

High and High Specific Intensity

The repetitions are increased for the exercises as previously, with the reps increasing from eight through to twelve in week three and beyond. The exercises that are measured by distance not reps are increased from 20m to 30m per exercise from week one through to three. The quality of each jump is increased

in any subseque'
that block.

Week 1: 8 reps
Week 2: 10 reps or ⌐
Week 3+: 12 reps or 30m/⌐

Maintenance

The stretch-shortening cycle can be maintained by performing the selected exercises without variations. It is therefore unnecessary to alter the training from week to week within this protocol.

RESISTANCE TRAINING

The objective of resistance training is to increase the athlete's slow speed, fast speed strength and musculature. The training also reduces the chances of injuries through creating stronger muscle and connective tissue, which provides enhanced protection to the joints.

Resistance Training Protocols

The different training protocols are combined to achieve all the resistance training benefits. Each protocol uses a selection of exercises in combination with different repetition and rest schemes to achieve the desired effects and optimize performance.

Preparation Protocol

This phase is used for athletes who are relatively new to resistance training. The protocol prepares the body for the stresses of training and allows time to learn the correct techniques for the exercises.

- Exercises: Squat, incline bench press, straight leg deadlift, bent over row, lunge,

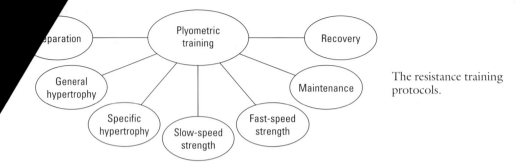

The resistance training protocols.

shoulder press, push and pull, cable twist, back raises and crunches.

- Order: Alternative (as written in the order above).
- Sets: 2/exercise.
- Reps: 15–5.
- Rest: 120sec.
- Lifting speed: Slow/medium.
- Technique: The sets are not performed to failure: each should be taken until the point of fatigue begins to inhibit technique.

General Hypertrophy Protocol

The objective of this protocol is to increase the all-round musculature of the athlete. This is achieved through using a variety of exercises that tax the major muscles.

- Exercises: Squat, straight leg deadlift, lunge, bent over row, chin-ups, back raises, push and pull, incline bench press, shoulder press, cable twists and crunch.
- Order: Consecutive (as written in the order above).
- Sets: 2/exercise.
- Reps: 12–6.
- Rest: 30–90sec.
- Lifting speed: Medium.
- Technique: Perform as many sets as possible to the point of failure within the bounds of correct technique.

Specific Hypertrophy Protocol

The protocol is designed to increase the size of the muscles specifically used during matches. It uses fewer exercises than the general hypertrophy protocol. The increase in size of the muscles that perform most of the work during matches allows for greater gains from the slow-speed strength protocol.

- Exercises: Straight leg deadlift, push and pull, squat, incline bench press, bent over row, lunge, cable twist, back raises and crunches.
- Sets: 3/exercise.
- Order: Alternative (as written in the order above).
- Reps: 12–6.
- Rest: 180sec.
- Lifting speed: Explosive.
- Technique: Perform all sets to the point of failure.

Slow-Speed Strength

Designed to increase the athlete's slow-speed strength. It targets the muscles that underlie performance on the rugby field, and increases their ability to produce the maximum amount of force.

- Exercises: Squat, incline bench press, straight-leg deadlift, bent over row.

- Order: Alternative (as written in the order above).
- Reps: 6–2.
- Sets: 4/exercise.
- Rest: 180sec.
- Lifting speed: Explosive.
- Technique: Do not perform the sets to the point of failure: stop on the repetition before the point you will need assistance. Ensure you are lifting the bar as quickly as possible.

Fast-Speed Strength

The aim of this protocol is to increase the amount of force that can be developed within 0.2sec. The exercises target the muscles predominantly used during competition, and involve lighter weights than the maximum strength protocol.

- Exercises: Jump squat, push and pull, lunge, cable twist, straight-leg deadlift, incline bench press and bent over row.
- Order: Alternative (as written in the order above).
- Sets: 3/exercise.
- Rest: 180 sec.
- Reps: 10–4.
- Lifting speed: Explosive.
- Technique: Perform the sets until explosiveness is lost. Use a weight that is lighter than one that you could handle maximally, e.g. for ten reps, use a true weight that could be lifted for fifteen reps.

Maintenance

The goal of the protocol is to maintain slow- and fast-speed strength along with muscular size. This is achieved by alternating two training sessions within the protocol.

STRENGTH SESSION:
- Exercises: Squat, push and pull, straight leg deadlift, cable twist.

- Order: Alternative (as written in the order above).
- Reps: 6.
- Sets: 4/exercise (2 sets fast-speed strength, 2 sets slow-speed strength).
- Rest: 180 sec.
- Lifting speed: Explosive.
- Technique: Use a lighter load than a true six rep max for the speed strength sets, e.g. true ten rep max. Then use the actual six rep max load for the strength sets.

HYPERTROPHY MAINTENANCE:
- Exercises: Squat, push and pull, straight leg deadlift, bent over row, cable twist, incline bench press, crunch, back raises.
- Order: Alternative (as written in the exercises above).
- Rest: 180sec.
- Reps: 6, 9, 12.
- Sets: 3/exercise.
- Lifting speed: Explosive.
- Technique: Failure should occur in all sets.

Recovery

Designed to help facilitate the body's recovery process. It uses a very light session that helps the central nervous system to recharge.

- Exercises: Squat, push and pull, lunge, cable twist, back raises, crunch.
- Order: Alternative (as above).
- Rest: 120 sec.
- Reps: 15.
- Sets: 2/exercise.
- Lifting speed: Medium.
- Technique: Use a weight that is lighter than maximal, e.g. a weight that can be lifted for twenty repetitions but perform just fifteen.

Progression of the Resistance Training Protocol

The individual protocols are progressed week by week through decreasing the number of repetitions and/or increasing the rest between sets. The weight lifted is changed in accordance with alterations of these parameters, and changes in the athlete's strength.

Preparation Protocol

The reps are decreased each week, starting from fifteen reps down to five reps in Week 3. The reps stay the same for a fourth week and all weeks after this, with the weight being increased when necessary.

Week 1: 15 reps/set
Week 2: 10 reps/set
Week 3+: 5 reps/set

INCREASING THE WEIGHT: In the first week perform fifteen reps, but with a weight that could be lifted for around eighteen reps if pushed to the limit. In the second week the weight is increased to that which could be lifted thirteen times if performed to failure, but perform only ten reps. The weight is again increased for the third week and thereafter using a weight that can be lifted eight times maximally but for just five reps.

To find the weight that should be used initially is trial and error. In addition to increasing the weight when the required number of reps is altered. With the body adapting to the stimulus it becomes necessary to increase the weight when the target rep number is being reached without any fatigue. Use a heavier load when you feel you could perform more than three repetitions above the target number.

Progression of the General Hypertrophy Protocol

The protocol is altered by simultaneously decreasing the number of reps while increasing the rest period between sets each week. If the protocol is performed over four weeks plus, continue with the Week 3 programme and increase the weight when necessary.

Week 1: 12 reps, 30sec rest
Week 2: 9 reps, 60sec rest
Week 3+: 6 reps, 90sec rest

INCREASING THE WEIGHT: The weight can be increased each time the training protocol requires fewer reps and more rest. The weight can also be increased when the target rep number is being achieved without reaching the point of failure.

Progression of the Specific Hypertrophy Protocol

The protocol keeps the rest between sets constant, but decreases the number of reps each week. The number of reps is kept at six if the block lasts for three weeks plus.

Week 1: 12 reps
Week 2: 9 reps
Week 3+: 6 reps

INCREASING THE WEIGHT: The weight is increased whenever the required number of reps is decreased, and when the target rep number is being achieved without reaching the point of failure.

Slow-Strength Protocol

The protocol is progressed by reducing the number of reps over the first three weeks. Any further weeks the reps remain constant and variation is provided by changing the weight.

Week 1:   6 reps
Week 2:   4 reps
Week 3+: 2 reps

INCREASING THE WEIGHT: The weight is increased when the target rep number is lowered, or when it can be reached without undue fatigue.

Fast-Speed Strength Protocol

The protocol is progressed through decreasing the number of repetitions performed.

Week 1:   10 reps
Week 2:   7 reps
Week 3+: 4 reps

INCREASING THE WEIGHT: The weights are increased whenever the repetitions are lowered; the increase should be done carefully, remembering that the weights used are lighter than those that could be handled maximally. Ensure the new weight is one that could be lifted for four or five reps more than the required number: for example, for four reps use an eight/nine rep maximum weight. The weight is *not* increased at any other times except when changing the number of required reps.

Maintenance

Maintaining muscle size, fast- and slow-speed strength can be achieved through performing the prescribed routines. The protocol does not need to be altered week to week.

INCREASING THE WEIGHT: Adjust the weight when necessary, either up or down, such that the target rep number is achieved.

Recovery Protocol

The recovery process is aided by performing the protocol without the need for it to be altered week to week.

INCREASING THE WEIGHT: Do not increase the weight during this protocol as the goal is to aid the recovery process rather than to challenge the body.

CORE TRAINING AND FLEXIBILITY

The goal of this training method is to increase a player's ability to hold the core stable during movement so that full force transfer can occur through the body, therefore optimizing performance. Flexibility training is performed to restore and maintain an ideal posture, which can reduce injuries and improve strength.

Core-Training Protocols

There are five core-training protocols. The exercises remain the same throughout them,

The core training protocols.

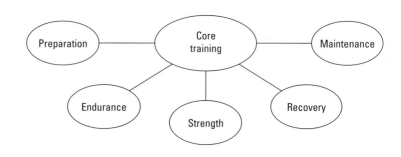

but the routine is changed. The exercises are based on time criteria instead of repetition.

Preparation

The aim of this protocol is to allow the athlete to familiarize themselves with the exercises, holding a neutral spine and engaging the core. The protocol begins to build a level of core strength.

- Exercises: Prone ball hold, ball bridge, side ball hold, ball twist.
- Order: Circuit training.
- Reps: 30–90sec.
- Sets: 1–2 /exercise.
- Rest: N/a.
- Technique: Ensure you have a neutral spine and do not go beyond the point at which this alignment is lost.

Endurance

The goal of this phase is to develop the ability of the muscles to hold the body in place for an extended duration.

- Exercises: Prone ball hold, ball bridge, side ball hold, ball twist.
- Order: Any.
- Reps: 120–150sec.
- Sets: 1/exercise.
- Rest: N/a.
- Technique: Ensure you have a neutral spine and do not go beyond the point at which this alignment is lost.

Strength

The goal of this phase is to develop the maximal ability of the core muscles to hold the mid-section in place.

- Exercises: Prone ball hold, ball bridge, side ball hold, ball twist.

- Order: Circuit training.
- Reps: 60–30sec.
- Sets: 2/exercise.
- Rest: N/a.
- Technique: Ensure you have a neutral spine and do not go beyond the point at which this alignment is lost.

Maintenance

The goal of this phase is to maintain both the endurance and strength of the core muscles.

- Exercises: Prone ball hold, ball bridge, side ball hold, ball twist.
- Order: Circuit training.
- Reps: 120 and 30sec.
- Sets: 2/exercise, 1 set for 30sec and 1 set for 120sec.
- Rest: N/a.
- Technique: Ensure you have a neutral spine and do not go beyond the point at which this alignment is lost.

Recovery

The goal of this phase is to aid the body's recovery mechanisms.

- Exercises: Prone ball hold, ball bridge, side ball hold, ball twist.
- Order: Circuit training.
- Reps: 30sec.
- Sets: 1/exercise.
- Rest: N/a.
- Technique: Perform at a comfortable intensity level. Ensure you have a neutral spine and do not go beyond the point at which this alignment is lost.

Progressing the Core-Training Protocols

The protocols are all progressed in the same manner, by changing the duration of the exercise, and the intensity when appropriate.

Preparation Protocol

The length of the exercise is increased week by week to develop a base level of endurance. The time is increased from 30 to 90sec over the first three weeks, and remains at 90sec thereafter. The difficulty of the exercise is increased whenever the time duration can be achieved without losing your neutral spine.

Week 1:   30sec/exercise
Week 2:   60sec/exercise
Week 3+: 90sec/exercise

Endurance Protocol

The exercise duration is increased each week to develop the endurance of the core muscles. The time is increased from 120 to 150sec over the first three weeks, where it remains thereafter. The difficulty of the exercise is increased whenever the time duration can be achieved without losing your neutral spine.

Week 1:   120sec/exercise
Week 2:   135sec/exercise
Week 3+: 150sec/exercise

Strength Protocol

The duration is decreased week by week to challenge your core strength. The time is decreased from 60 to 30sec over the first three weeks, and remains at 30sec thereafter. The difficulty of the exercise is increased whenever the duration of the exercise is shortened, or if the desired time can be achieved without losing your neutral spine.

Week 1:   60sec/exercise
Week 2:   45sec/exercise
Week 3+: 30sec/exercise

Maintenance

The maintenance protocol is not progressed by changing the programme. However, the intensity of the exercises should be adjusted as necessary to ensure the goal time is being reached as fatigue sets in.

Recovery

A gentle intensity level is used to aid recovery. There are no weekly progressions within the protocol.

Flexibility Protocols and Progression

Flexibility training does not have protocols or progressions. This training should be performed all year round and wherever possible, for example before and after training, at home watching television, while recovering from injury, and so on.

It is important to do the stretch tests regularly to see what areas to focus your stretching on. All the given stretches should be performed regardless of the results from the tests, but extra emphasis should be placed on the muscles that cause you to fail the tests.

APPLYING THE TRAINING PROTOCOLS TO THE YEARLY STRUCTURE

The blocks within the off-season and in-season each have a protocol applied to them from the six training methods. The protocols are set out so that the overall training manipulates the training variables and stress as according to the principles of periodization: that is, increasing the intensity over the course of the off-season, and so on.

Applying the Training Protocols to the Off-Season

The off-season is the time when fitness levels are increased to the greatest extent. A different protocol is used in each of the five off-season training blocks (*see* Table 10).

Applying the Protocols to the In-season

When deciding on the training protocol to be used, the in-season is more complicated than the off-season. The in-season is divided into maintenance, recovery and development blocks (*see* Table 11). In the recovery and maintenance blocks the corresponding protocol of the same name is used if applicable.

The development block uses the same training protocol as during the off-season. A single week of training from the different protocols is performed. How many of these weeks are performed depends upon the length of the development block.

The application of the training weeks is done so that the individual weeks are applied in the reverse order to that in which they were performed during the off-season (*see* Table 12).

The development blocks act as mini off-seasons. They allow improvements in your physical attributes to occur during periods of the in-season when no important fixtures take place. To best illustrate how the protocols are applied to the training blocks throughout the year, each of the six training methods can be examined.

TABLE 10: APPLICATION OF THE TRAINING PROTOCOL TO THE OFF-SEASON

Off-season Recovery	*Base-fitness preparation*	*General fitness preparation*	*Sport-specific preparation*	*Position-specific preparation*
No formal training	Protocol 1	Protocol 2	Protocol 3	Protocol 4

TABLE 11: APPLICATION OF TRAINING PROTOCOL TO THE IN-SEASON

In-season Maintenance	*Rec*	*Maintenance*	*Dev*	*Maintenance*	*Dev*
Maintenance	Rec	Maintenance	See Table 12	Maintenance	See Table 12

Applying the Aerobic Endurance Protocols to the Year

Off-Season

After the recovery block, where no training takes place, the intensity of the exercises is gradually increased through the off-season. This is achieved by placing the steady pace protocol first, followed by intervals with recovery, then intervals with rest. The off-season ends with special endurance training to fine tune the player's aerobic power and lactate tolerance in time for the opening day of the season (*see* Table 13).

The weekly progressions for each protocol are applied within these blocks to finalize the

aerobic endurance training to be used in the off-season.

In-Season

The maintenance and recovery protocols are applied to their correspondingly named blocks. How to implement the training protocol to the development block is dependent upon its length (*see* Tables 14 and 15).

A three-week development block during the in-season would consist of the athlete performing intervals with recovery in the first week, then intervals with rest in the second week, followed by special endurance training in the third and final week of the development block. The athlete performs the training protocols

---

**TABLE 12: APPLICATION OF TRAINING PROTOCOLS
TO THE IN-SEASON'S DEVELOPMENT BLOCK**

Length of development block	Off-season training protocol employed (1st week, 2nd week, 3rd week, . . .)
1 week	Protocol (4)
2 weeks	Protocol (3), Protocol (4)
3 weeks	Protocol (2), Protocol (3), Protocol (4)
4 weeks	Protocol (1), Protocol (2), Protocol (3), Protocol (4)
5 weeks	Protocol (1), Protocol (2), Protocol (3), Protocol (4) × 2 weeks

---

**TABLE 13: APPLICATION OF THE AEROBIC ENDURANCE
TRAINING PROTOCOL TO THE OFF-SEASON**

Off-season Recovery	Base fitness preparation	General fitness preparation	Sport-specific preparation	Position-specific preparation
No formal training	Steady pace	Intervals and recovery	Intervals and rest	Special endurance

TABLE 14: APPLICATION OF THE AEROBIC TRAINING PROTOCOL TO THE IN-SEASON

In-season Maintenance	Rec	Maintenance	Dev	Maintenance	Dev
Maintenance	Rec	Maintenance	See Table 15	Maintenance	See Table 15

TABLE 15: APPLICATION OF THE AEROBIC ENDURANCE TRAINING PROTOCOLS TO A DEVELOPMENT BLOCK OF THE IN-SEASON

Length of development block	Off-season training protocol employed (1st week, 2nd week, 3rd week, . . .)
1 week	Special endurance
2 weeks	Intervals & recovery, special endurance
3 weeks	Intervals & recovery, intervals & rest, special endurance
4 weeks	Steady pace, intervals & recovery, intervals & rest, special endurance
5 weeks	Steady pace, intervals and recovery, intervals and rest, special endurance × 2 weeks

using the first week's routine of each block; for example, 3min: 1min × 5 for intervals with recovery (*see* Chapter 8 for the specific training performed in the individual weeks).

Applying the Sprint-Training Protocols to the Year

Off-Season

The off-season represents the time to make the greatest gains in sprinting abilities. After the recovery block, where no formal training is performed, the sprint-training protocols are placed in decreasing distance across the blocks. The 300m protocol is followed by the 200m, which is succeeded by the 100m, then 0–60m protocols. This decreasing distance (volume) allows for higher training intensities to be used, which maximizes responses to the training (*see* Table 16).

The weekly progressions are then applied to the individual training protocols within the blocks to complete the training routine for the off-season.

The In-Season

The maintenance and recovery blocks use the protocols of the same name. The application of sprint training to the in-season development blocks varies according to its length (*see* Tables 17 and 18).

TABLE 16: APPLICATION OF THE SPRINT-TRAINING PROTOCOL TO THE OFF-SEASON

Off-season Recovery	Base fitness preparation	General fitness preparation	Sport-specific preparation	Position-specific preparation
No formal training	300m	200m	100m	0–60m

TABLE 17: APPLICATION OF THE SPRINT-TRAINING PROTOCOL TO THE IN-SEASON

In-season Maintenance	Rec	Maintenance	Dev	Maintenance	Dev
Maintenance	Rec	Maintenance	See Table 18	Maintenance	See Table 18

TABLE 18: APPLICATION OF THE SPRINT-TRAINING PROTOCOL TO THE DEVELOPMENT BLOCK OF THE IN-SEASON

Length of development block	Off-season training protocol employed (1st week, 2nd week, 3rd week, . . .)
1 week	0–60m
2 weeks	100m, 0–60m
3 weeks	200m, 100m, 0–60m
4 weeks	300m, 200m, 100m, 0–60m
5 weeks	300m, 200m, 100m, 0–60m × 2 weeks

In a four-week development block, the athlete would perform 300m in the first week, 200m in the second week, 100m in the third and 0–60m sprints in the fourth and final week of the block. The first week's training routine would be followed for each protocol; for example, in week two, 4 × 200m with 3min rest.

Applying the Agility Training Protocol to the Year

Off-Season

After performing no training during the initial recovery block, the protocols are then placed so they perform progressively more complex movements over the course of the off-season. The agility training starts with foundation movements, then employs the basic movement exercises. Increasingly challenging exercises are performed with the combination movements protocol, followed finally by the rugby-specific movements. This ensures that the intensity and specificity of the exercises are increased during the off-season (*see* Table 19).

The weekly progressions are applied to each protocol within the blocks to complete the agility routine.

In-Season

The maintenance protocol is employed during the maintenance blocks, while no agility training is performed during a recovery block. The development block's training protocol is determined by its length (*see* Tables 20 and 21).

A two-week development block would use the combination movement exercise protocol in the first week, followed by the rugby-specific movement exercises in the second and final week of the block. The first week's routines for the protocols are used in each: for example, Week 1 perform 5m or 25m per combination exercise.

Applying the Plyometric Training Protocol to the Year

Off-Season

There is no training during the initial block of the off-season. The plyometric training then gradually increases the intensity and specificity of the exercises over the course of the off-season. The protocols followed are dependent upon whether the athlete fulfils the criteria for high intensity plyometrics.

In the first two blocks the player performs low, then medium intensity exercise. He then performs high intensity and high intensity specific exercises, if he fulfils the required criteria. If not, he performs another block of the medium intensity exercises, followed by medium intensity specific (*see* Tables 22 and 23).

The weekly progressions are applied to the training protocol within each block to finalize the training routine.

TABLE 19: APPLICATION OF THE AGILITY TRAINING PROTOCOL TO THE OFF-SEASON

Off-season Recovery	Base fitness preparation	General fitness preparation	Sport-specific preparation	Position-specific preparation
No formal training	Foundation movements	Basic movements	Combination movements	Rugby-specific movements

TABLE 20: APPLICATION OF THE AGILITY TRAINING PROTOCOL TO THE IN-SEASON

In-season Maintenance	Rec	Maintenance	Dev	Maintenance	Dev
Maintenance	Rec	Maintenance	See Table 21	Maintenance	See Table 21

TABLE 21: APPLICATION OF THE AGILITY TRAINING PROTOCOL TO THE DEVELOPMENT BLOCK OF THE IN-SEASON

Length of development block	Off-season training protocol employed (1st week, 2nd week, 3rd week, . . .)
1 week	Rugby-specific movements
2 weeks	Combination movements, rugby-specific movements
3 weeks	Basic movements, combination movements, rugby-specific movements
4 weeks	Foundation movements, basic movements, combination movements, rugby-specific movements
5 weeks	Foundation movements, basic movements, combination movements, rugby-specific movements × 2 weeks

TABLE 22: APPLICATION OF THE PLYOMETRIC TRAINING PROTOCOL TO THE OFF-SEASON FOR PLAYERS WHO FULFIL THE CRITERIA TO PERFORM HIGH INTENSITY EXERCISES

Off-season Recovery	Base fitness preparation	General fitness preparation	Sport-specific preparation	Position-specific preparation
No formal training	Low intensity	Medium intensity	High intensity	High intensity specific

TABLE 23: APPLICATION OF THE PLYOMETRIC TRAINING PROTOCOL
TO THE OFF-SEASON FOR PLAYERS WHO DO NOT FULFIL THE
CRITERIA TO PERFORM HIGH INTENSITY EXERCISES

Off-season Recovery	Base fitness preparation	General fitness preparation	Sport-specific preparation	Position-specific preparation
No formal training	Low intensity	Medium intensity	High intensity	High intensity specific

In-Season

The maintenance protocol is employed during the maintenance blocks, while no plyometric training is performed during a recovery block. The development blocks' training protocol is dependent upon the length of the block (*see* Tables 24 and 25).

A three-week development block for an athlete who does not meet the high intensity plyometric criteria would see the athlete in the first two weeks performing medium intensity plyometrics. In the third and final week, medium specific exercises would be used. The first and second weeks' training for the medium intensity protocol is performed – for example, eight and ten reps in weeks one and two – followed by the first week's training protocol of the medium intensity specific exercises, for example eight reps.

Applying Resistance Training Protocol to the Year

Off-Season

The recovery block has no resistance training protocol performed. The structuring of the protocols through the remaining blocks is dependent upon whether the athlete meets the slow-speed strength criteria. It is required

to have at least one year's experience of regularly lifting weights before performing this type of training.

If the criteria are met the general hypertrophy is succeeded by the specific hypertrophy. Slow-speed strength training then follows, with fast-speed strength training completing the off-season.

When the criteria is not met to perform maximum strength training a preparation block is first performed, followed by the general, then the specific hypertrophy protocols. Finally, fast-speed strength is placed in the remaining block of the off-season (*see* Tables 26 and 27).

The weekly progressions and weight alterations are then applied to the individual weeks of each protocol.

In-Season

The maintenance and recovery phases use the correspondingly named protocol, while the development block uses different protocol, dependent upon the length of the block and whether the athlete is able to perform slow-speed strength training (*see* Tables 28 and 29).

A five-week development block would require the player who meets the maximum strength criteria to perform general, then

TABLE 24: APPLICATION OF THE PLYOMETRIC TRAINING PROTOCOL TO THE IN-SEASON

In-season Maintenance	Rec	Maintenance	Dev	Maintenance	Dev
Maintenance	Rec	Maintenance	See Table 25	Maintenance	See Table 25

TABLE 25: APPLICATION OF THE PLYOMETRIC TRAINING PROTOCOL TO THE DEVELOPMENT BLOCK OF THE IN-SEASON

Length of development block	Off-season training protocol employed (1st week, 2nd week, 3rd week, . . .)
1 week	High specific (medium specific)*
2 weeks	High (medium)*, High specific (medium specific)*
3 weeks	Medium, high (medium specific × 2 weeks)*, High specific
4 weeks	Low, medium, high (medium specific × 2 weeks)*, High specific
5 weeks	Low, medium, high (medium)*, high specific × 2 weeks, (medium specific × 2 weeks)*

* To be performed if player does not meet the criteria for high intensity exercises.

TABLE 26: APPLICATION OF THE TRAINING PROTOCOLS TO THE OFF-SEASON FOR AN ATHLETE WHO PERFORMS SLOW-SPEED STRENGTH TRAINING

Off-season Recovery	Base fitness preparation	General fitness preparation	Sport-specific preparation	Position-specific preparation
No formal preparation	General hypertrophy	Specific hypertrophy	Slow-speed strength	Fast-speed strength

TABLE 27: APPLICATION OF THE TRAINING PROTOCOLS TO THE OFF-SEASON FOR AN ATHLETE WHO DOES NOT MEET THE CRITERIA TO PERFORM MAXIMUM STRENGTH TRAINING

Off-season Recovery	Base fitness preparation	General fitness preparation	Sport-specific preparation	Position-specific preparation
No formal training	Preparation	General hypertrophy	Specific hypertrohy	Fast-speed strength

TABLE 28: APPLICATION OF THE RESISTANCE TRAINING PROTOCOL TO THE IN-SEASON

In-season Maintenance	Rec	Maintenance	Dev	Maintenance	Dev
Maintenance	Rec	Maintenance	See Table 29	Maintenance	See Table 29

TABLE 29: APPLICATION OF THE RESISTANCE TRAINING PROTOCOL TO THE DEVELOPMENT BLOCK OF THE IN-SEASON

Length of development block	Off-season training protocol employed
1 week	Fast-speed strength
2 weeks	Slow-speed strength (specific hyp*), fast-speed strength
3 weeks	Specific hyp (general hyp*), slow-speed strength (specific hyp*), fast-speed strength
4 weeks	General hyp (preparation*), specific hyp (general hyp*) slow-speed strength (specific hyp*), fast-speed strength.
5 weeks	General hyp (preparation*), specific hyp (general hyp*) slow-speed strength (specific hyp*), fast-speed strength × 2 weeks

* To be performed if player does not meet the criteria for maximum strength training.

specific hypertrophy, in weeks one and two of the block. In Week 3 he would perform slow-speed strength training before completing two weeks of fast-speed strength. Each of the phases would use the first week training of the protocol except for the fast-speed strength, where he would use both Week 1 and Week 2 of the weekly progressions: for example, performing ten reps in Week 4, and seven reps in Week 5 of the development block.

Applying the Core Conditioning Protocols to the Year

Off-Season

After the recovery block, where no specific core exercises are performed, the preparation protocol is followed during the base fitness block. The general fitness preparation block uses the endurance protocol. The sport- and position-specific blocks both use the strength protocol (*see* Table 30).

The weekly changes and exercise progressions are then applied to the individual weeks within each protocol.

In-Season

The maintenance and recovery protocols are used with their respective named blocks. The protocols used in the development blocks depend upon the duration of each one (*see* Tables 31 and 32).

A three-week development block would require the player to perform the preparation protocol in week one. In Week 2 he would perform the endurance protocol, before performing strength protocol in Week 3. Each of the phases would use the first week training of

---

TABLE 30: APPLICATION OF THE CORE TRAINING PROTOCOLS TO THE OFF-SEASON

Off-season Recovery	Base fitness preparation	General fitness preparation	Sport-specific preparation	Position-specific preparation
No formal training	Preparation protocol	Endurance protocol	Strength protocol	Strength protocol

---

TABLE 31: APPLICATION OF THE CORE TRAINING PROTOCOLS TO THE IN-SEASON

In-season Maintenance	Rec	Maintenance	Dev	Maintenance	Dev
Maintenance	Rec	Maintenance	See Table 32	Maintenance	See Table 32

TABLE 32: APPLICATION OF THE RESISTANCE TRAINING PROTOCOL TO THE DEVELOPMENT

Length of development block	Off-season training protocol employed (1st week, 2nd week, 3rd week, . . .)
1 week	Strength
2 weeks	Endurance, strength
3 weeks	Preparation, endurance, strength
4 weeks	Preparation, endurance, strength × 2 weeks
5 weeks	Preparation, endurance × 2 weeks, strength × 2 weeks

the protocol; for example, in Week 2 he would perform the core exercises for 120sec.

Applying Flexibility Training to the Year

Flexibility training should be performed all year round, regardless of what block the athlete is in. It is vital to ensure adequate flexibility, so use the stretch tests regularly to guide you where to give extra attention with your stretching.

Weekly Structure

You now have the knowledge to align the protocols with the training blocks. The final area that needs to be examined is how and when the exercises within each training method can be performed during the week.

The training methods need not all be performed separately as individual sessions, but may instead be combined where possible to save time. The methods can be separated into three training sessions (*see* Table 34).

The sessions are arranged such that fatigue does not affect the subsequent method used; for example, resistance and aerobic training are performed separately, as each would inhibit the effect of the other. Session A is able to combine three methods as they do not interfere with subsequent methods.

The training sessions A, B and C are performed either once, twice, or not at all during a week, depending on the training block.

Weekly Layout

The arrangement of the training sessions plays a vital role in the overall success of the training programme: they are applied sequentially during the week in the order given (session A, then B, then C), therefore maximizing the time between the same type of training session (*see* Table 35).

The off-day can be placed anywhere in the week dependent upon personal circumstances (*see* Tables 36 and 37).

If it is more suitable to train twice a day, then it is important to apply the sessions in the same order also (session A, then B, then C) to ensure that fatigue from one session does not affect the following session (*see* Table 38).

Allowing for Competitive Matches

The in-season contains the team's competitive fixtures, and a game is scheduled most weeks. To prepare and recover from this a rest day should be placed the day before and after the match. This ensures the player is fresh to play, and is then given time to recover from the demands of competition (*see* Table 39).

TABLE 33: SUMMARY OF THE INDIVIDUAL TRAINING SESSIONS

Training session	Training methods performed	Length of session
Session A	Agility, plyometrics and sprint training	30–90min
Session B	Resistance and core training	30–90min
Session C	Aerobic endurance training	20–40min

TABLE 34: NUMBER OF TRAINING SESSIONS PERFORMED DURING EACH TRAINING BLOCK

Season	Training block	Number of sessions performed /week		
		Session A	Session B	Session C
	Recovery	0	0	0
	Base fitness training	2	2	2
	General fitness preparation	2	2	2
Off-season	Sports-specific preparation	2	2	2
	Position-specific preparation	2	2	2
	Maintenance	1	2	1
In-season	Development	2	2	2
	Recovery	1	1	1

TABLE 35: PLACEMENT OF THE TRAINING SESSIONS WITHIN A WEEK

Mon	Tues	Wed	Thurs	Fri	Sat	Sun
Session A	Session B	Session C	Session A	Session B	Session C	Off

TABLE 36: PLACEMENT OF THE TRAINING SESSIONS WITHIN A WEEK

Mon	Tues	Wed	Thurs	Fri	Sat	Sun
Session A	Session B	Session C	Off	Session A	Session B	Session C

The sessions' layout during a week should ideally be placed in the ABC order described: session A, then B, then C. This order optimizes recovery from training. If this is not possible, then sessions should still be performed. The benefits of doing the sessions, as compared to missing one, far outweigh the difference between using the ideal session order or not.

Rest

There should always be at least one rest day a week, and two if a competitive fixture is scheduled. This allows the body time to recover, helping to keep you from overtraining.

It is also essential that you have at least one day's break between performing the same

TABLE 37: ALLOWING FOR TEAM TRAINING SESSIONS INTO THE WEEKLY LAYOUT

Mon	Tues	Wed	Thurs	Fri	Sat	Sun
Session B	Session A Team training	Session C	Session B Team training	Session B	Session C	Off

TABLE 38: ALLOWING FOR TEAM TRAINING SESSIONS INTO THE WEEKLY LAYOUT

Mon	Tues	Wed	Thurs	Fri	Sat	Sun
Session A Session B	Session C Team training	Off	Session A Team training	Session B Session C	Off	Off

TABLE 39: WEEKLY LAYOUT DURING THE WEEKS OF IN-SEASON WHERE A MATCH IS SCHEDULED

Mon	Tues	Wed	Thurs	Fri	Sat	Sun
Session A	Session B Team training	Session C	Session A Team training	Off	Game	Off

type of training session; for instance, do not perform a resistance training session on Monday, then repeat on Tuesday. The body would not have recovered from the Monday if you did this, therefore making the second session a waste of your efforts; it also increases your chances of injury and overtraining.

Attendance

It may not be possible to perform all the pre-scribed number of sessions due to other com-mitments. This should not cause too much worry, as you are bound by your personal cir-cumstances.

When unable to meet the desired number of each session type in a week, try to ensure that you keep rotating them so you perform the training sessions sequentially through the weeks. For instance, if you can perform four sessions a week, in Week 1 do Session A, B, C, A, then in Week 2 session B, C, A, B, and so on.

Training before work/college is an effec-tive way to find room for these training ses-sions, allowing you to train twice a day, and it sets you up perfectly for the day ahead.

The design of the week does allow for some flexibility, depending upon personal schedule and preference. However, where at all possi-ble the rules above should be observed.

Individual Session Structure

The individual sessions within the week are comprised of a warm-up, a main session, and a cool-down.

The Warm-Up

The warm-up consists of:
- Five minutes gentle activity, e.g. light jog, bike, etc., followed by, . . .
- . . . for sessions A and C, two sets of the sprint technique drills.

. . . for session B, perform the exercises with a lighter weight first.

The Main Session

The sessions should follow the protocol set out previously. For session A, perform the routine in the following order:

1st   agility protocol
2nd   plyometrics protocol
3rd   sprint training protocol

This structure ensures that the effect of fatigue on the following method is kept to a minimum.

For session B, perform the routine in the following order:

1st   resistance training
2nd   core conditioning

The Cool-Down

Following the main session, a cool-down is performed. The cool-down is important, as it helps in the removal of lactic acid, restores mental calm, and ensures the muscles maintain flexibility. The cool-down is structured thus:
- Perform a 5min light aerobic activity, for example a gentle jog, walk or cycle.
- Perform static stretching using all the stretches given, but paying particular attention to the body parts that were diag-nosed tight in the stretch tests.

SUMMARY

The six training methods have now been explained. The previous sections have shown the different protocols, how they are pro-gressed from week to week, and when to apply them within the year. The weekly and session layouts have been defined. You now have the knowledge needed to design your own training programme.

CHAPTER 7

Designing Your Personal Training Programme

You are now ready to design your own programme, and this chapter takes you through the ten steps that will give you a year-long conditioning programme. Time should be taken to carefully review the ten steps. In the Appendix, blank forms and reference tables can be found for you to use; this will give you all the material and knowledge you need to plan your programme for a year in advance.

STEP 1: PLACING TODAY'S DATE ON THE CHART

Using a pencil, insert the date for the beginning of each week on to the chart (*see* Table 40).

STEP 2: PLACING THE OFF-/IN-SEASON

Place the start and finish of the current season, and the next season afterwards. Mark where the off-season and in-season begin (*see* Table 41).

STEP 3: PLANNING THE OFF-SEASON

The off-season needs to be divided into the five blocks, with recovery weeks where necessary. Begin by placing a two-week recovery block (Rec) at the beginning of the off-season, and a recovery week at the end of the off-season (*see* Table 42).

Now place a recovery week in the middle of the off-season: if there is an odd number of weeks, place the recovery week so there are more weeks at the beginning of the period than at the end (*see* Table 43).

Now divide each of the two halves into the remaining four training blocks, with the larger blocks being earlier in the off-season. Label each of these blocks as follows: base fitness, general fitness, sport- and position-specific preparation (*see* Table 44).

Starting your Programme During the Off-Season

If the start of your training programme occurs during the off-season, then there may be

	TABLE 40: PLACING THE DATE ON THE CHART									
Week	*Apr*	*Apr*	*Apr*	*Apr*	*May*	*May*	*May*	*May*	*May*	*June*	*June*
	3	10	17	24	1	8	15	22	29	5	12

TABLE 41: APPLYING THE OFF-/IN-SEASON TO THE TRAINING CHART

Week	Apr	Apr	Apr	Apr	May	May	May	May	May	June	June
	3	10	17	24	1	8	15	22	29	5	12
	In-season				Off-season						

TABLE 42: APPLYING THE RECOVERY WEEKS TO THE OFF-SEASON

April		May					June				July				August			
19	26	3	10	17	24	31	7	14	21	28	5	12	19	26	2	9	16	23
Rec	Rec																	Rec

TABLE 43: APPLYING EXTRA RECOVERY WEEKS TO THE OFF-SEASON

April		May					June				July				August			
19	26	3	10	17	24	31	7	14	21	28	5	12	19	26	2	9	16	23
Rec	Rec									Rec								Rec

TABLE 44: APPLYING THE TRAINING BLOCKS TO THE OFF-SEASON

April		May					June				July				August			
19	26	3	10	17	24	31	7	14	21	28	5	12	19	26	2	9	16	23
Rec	Rec	Base fitness preparation					General fitness preparation			Rec	Sport-specific preparation				Position-specific preparation			Rec

insufficient time to complete the full programme as described above.

If the start of your training programme leaves you with less than fifteen weeks' training time before the beginning of the next in-season, structure the blocks as according to Table 45.

The next off-season after this shortened season will allow time to complete the whole training programme as described previously.

STEP 4: TRANSFERRING THE TRAINING PROTOCOL

With the blocks in place, transfer the correct training types used into each of the six training methods, as discussed in the last chapter (*see* Table 46).

When using the shortened off-season structure, the protocol should be employed in accordance to the general patterns described

TABLE 45: THE OFF-SEASON STRUCTURE FOR AN OFF-SEASON DURATION OF FIFTEEN WEEKS OR LESS

Length of off-season	May			June				July				August			
	17	24	31	7	14	21	28	5	12	19	26	2	9	16	23
15 weeks	R	B			Gen			R	SS			PS			R
14 weeks	–	R	B			Gen		R	SS			PS			R
13 weeks	–	–	R	B			Gen		R	SS		PS			R
12 weeks	–	–	–	R	B		Gen		R	SS		PS			R
11 weeks	–	–	–	–	R	B	Gen		R	SS		PS			R
10 weeks	–	–	–	–	–	R	B		Gen	SS		PS			R
9 weeks	–	–	–	–	–	–	R	B		Gen		SS			R
8 weeks	–	–	–	–	–	–	–	R	B		Gen	SS			R
7 weeks	–	–	–	–	–	–	–	–	R	B				Gen	R
6 weeks	–	–	–	–	–	–	–	–	–	B				Gen	R
5 weeks	–	–	–	–	–	–	–	–	–	–	–	B		Gen	R
4 weeks	–	–	–	–	–	–	–	–	–	–	–	–	B		R
3 weeks	–	–	–	–	–	–	–	–	–	–	–	–	B	B	R
2 weeks	–	–	–	–	–	–	–	–	–	–	–	–	–	B	R
1 week	–	–	–	–	–	–	–	–	–	–	–	–	–	–	R

Key: B – Base fitness preparation, Gen – General fitness preparation, SS – Sport-specific training, PS – Position-specific preparation, R – Recovery.

TABLE 46: APPLYING THE TRAINING PROTOCOL TO THE TRAINING BLOCKS

April		May					June			July				August			
19	26	3	10	17	24	31	7	14	21	28	5	12	19	26	2	9	16	23
Recovery		Base fitness preparation					General fitness preparation			Rec	Sport-specific preparation				Position-specific preparation			Rec
No formal training		Steady pace					Intervals recovery			Recovery training	Intervals & rest				Special endurance			Recovery training
		300m					200m				100m				0–60m			
		Foundation movements					Basic movements				Combination movements				Rugby specific			
		Low					Medium				High (medium)*				High specific (medium)*			
		General hyp (prep)*					Specific hyp (General hyp)*				Max strength (Specific hyp)*				Speed Strength			
		Preparation					Endurance				Strength				Strength			

*To be used if criteria not met for other training protocol.

above and in Chapter 6. The shortened blocks may only allow progression over two weeks (*see* Table 47).

Even shorter off-season lengths result in many training blocks and protocols not being used at all. An example of a six-week off-season is shown below (*see* Table 48).

STEP 5: PLANNING THE IN-SEASON

The in-season is a little more difficult to plan in advance: first, schedule a recovery week every ten weeks, then place the development blocks where there are no games scheduled at the time of writing (*see* Table 49).

This gives a provisional structure of maintenance, recovery and development blocks. It is only provisional, as the cancellation of fixtures and non-involvement with games may create more development weeks. Alternatively, the rescheduling of matches to free weekends may remove a development block.

Creating more Development and Recovery Blocks

A full fixture calendar often leaves little room for developing fitness through long maintenance training blocks. In these circumstances, a development week can be scheduled, despite the presence of a game that week. The development blocks should be placed when a

141

TABLE 47: APPLYING THE TRAINING PROTOCOL TO THE TRAINING BLOCKS OF A TWELVE-WEEK OFF-SEASON

May			June				July				August			
17	24	31	7	14	21	28	5	12	19	26	2	9	16	23
–	–	–	Rec	Base fitness			General fitness		Rec	Sport-specific		Position-specific		Rec
–	–	–	No formal training	Steady Pace			Intervals recovery		Recovery training	Intervals & rest		Special endurance		Recovery training
–	–	–		300m			200m			100m		0–60m		
–	–	–		Foundation movements			Basic movements			Combination movements		Rugby-specific movements		
–	–	–		Low			Medium			High (med)*		High Specific (med)*		
–	–	–		General hyp (prep)*			Specific hyp (Gen hyp)*			Max strength (Spec hyp)*		Speed Strength		
–	–	–		Preparation			End			Strength		Strength		

*To be used if criteria not met for other training protocol.

fixture is relatively unimportant – for instance, a friendly – as the extra training may diminish performance.

When injury prevents participation in a game, then development protocol may be followed within the limits of the injury; for example, a thumb injury will allow all training to be performed except resistance training.

It may be necessary to insert extra recovery weeks if you are feeling tired from the continual training. It is essential you have enough recovery, or you will suffer from overtraining.

When to add these extra blocks is down to your own discretion, but I would advise caution on inserting too many extra development blocks, especially without the addition of recovery weeks.

STEP 6: TRANSFERRING THE TRAINING PROTOCOL

The planned training blocks within the in-season can now be matched to the appropriate training protocol to assign the conditioning routines (see Tables 50, 51, 52 and 53).

TABLE 48: APPLYING THE TRAINING PROTOCOL TO THE TRAINING BLOCKS OF A SIX-WEEK OFF-SEASON

July		August			
19	26	2	9	16	23
Base fitness preparation		General fitness preparation			Recovery
Steady pace		Intervals & recovery			Recovery training
300m		200m			
Basic movement		Combination movement			
Low		Medium			
General hyp (prep)*		Specific hyp (Gen hyp)*			
Preparation		Endurance			

*To be used if criteria not met for other training protocol.

TABLE 49: APPLYING THE TRAINING BLOCKS TO THE IN-SEASON

Sept					Oct				Nov				Dec				Jan					Feb				Mar				Apr	
30	6	13	20	27	4	11	18	25	1	8	15	22	29	6	15	20	27	3	10	17	24	31	7	14	21	28	7	14	21	28	4	11
M									R	D				M		D	M		R	M			D			M				D	M

Key: D – Development, M – Maintenance, R – Recovery.

143

TABLE 50: APPLICATION OF THE TRAINING PROTOCOL TO THE IN-SEASON TRAINING BLOCKS

	Sept					Oct				Nov					Dec				Jan					Feb				Mar				Apr	
	30	6	13	20	27	4	11	18	25	1	8	15	22	29	6	15	20	27	3	10	17	24	31	7	14	21	28	7	14	21	28	4	11
Maintenance										R	D		M		D	M			R	M				D		M						D	M
Maintenance protocol										R	See Table 49		M		See Table 49	M			R	M				See Table 49		M						See Table 49	M

Key: D – Development, M – Maintenance, R – Recovery.

TABLE 51: TRAINING PROTOCOL OF THE THREE-WEEK DEVELOPMENT BLOCK

Week	Training protocol for each training method
15–21 November	Intervals & recovery, medium intensity plymetrics*, 200m, basic movements agility, general hypertrophy**, preparation core exercises.
22–28 November	Intervals with rest, high intensity plyometrics*, 100m, combination movements agility, specific hypertrophy, endurance core exercises.
29 November–3 December	Special endurance, high intensity specific plyometrics*, 0–60m, rugby-specific movements agility, speed strengh**, strength core exercises.

*Assuming athletes meet criteria for high intensity plyometrics.
**Assuming athlete does not meet criteria to perform maximum strength training.

TABLE 52: TRAINING PROTOCOL OF THE ONE-WEEK DEVELOPMENT BLOCK

Week	Training protocol for each training method:
20–26 December	Special endurance, high intensity specific plyometrics*, 0–60m, rugby-specific movements, agility, fast-speed strength**, strength core exercises.

*Assuming athletes meet criteria for high intensity plyometrics.
**Assuming athlete does not meet criteria to perform maximum strength training.

TABLE 53: TRAINING PROTOCOL OF THE TWO-WEEK DEVELOPMENT BLOCK

Week	Training protocol for each training method
7–13 February	Intervals & rest, high intensity specific plyometrics*, 0–60m, rugby-specific movements agility, fast-speed strength**, strength core exercises.
14–20 February	Special endurance, high intensity plyometrics*, 100m, combination movement agility, specific hypertrophy**. Endurance core exercises.

*Assuming athletes meet criteria for high intensity plyometrics.
**Assuming athletes do not meet criteria to perform maximum strength training.

STEP 7: IMPLEMENTING THE PROGRAMME

The training protocols have now been provisionally set out. Using the relevant tables found in the Appendix, the beginning of each training block can be provisionally set out. Use this example and Chapter 8 to guide you (see Table 54).

Period: In-season
Block: Maintenance
Dates: 15 March–4 April
Number of weeks: 3

Notes:

TABLE 54: WEEKLY LAYOUT FOR A TRAINING BLOCK

Mon	Tues	Wed	Thurs	Fri	Sat	Sun
Session B	Session A Team training	Session C	Session B Team training	Off	Game	Off

Training Protocol

Aerobic Endurance Training

Special endurance 100m course × 20.

Sprint Training

1 × 20, 40, 60, 100, 250, 5min rest.

Agility Training

Combination and rugby-specific movements, 1 rep/exercise (5m and 25m for combination movements, 10m and 25m for rugby-specific exercises).

Plyometric Training

High intensity specific 1 × 8 reps/exercise, 90sec rest.

Resistance Training

Session 1: Bench press, squats, bent over row, deadlifts.
4 sets/exercise of 6* reps with 120sec rest between sets.
Session 2: Squat, bench press incline, deadlift, bent over row, shoulder press, chins.
3 sets/exercise of 6, 9, 12 reps, 180sec rest.

Core Conditioning

Maintenance exercises: 1 × 30sec and 1 × 120sec /exercise.

Attendance summary (Number of Weeks: 3):
Session A: 3/3
Session B: 6/6
Session C: 3/3
Team Practice: 4/6
Game: 3/3

Notes: Played well, did some great tackles. I feel really strong.

*Using 6 rep max for 2 sets, and a lighter weight (true 10 rep max) for 2 sets.

TABLE 55: PLACING THE TESTING DATES DURING THE TRAINING YEAR

Mar	Apr	May	Jun	Jul	Aug	Sept	Oct	Nov	Dec	Jan	Feb
In-season	Off-season					In-season					
		T				T		T			T

T – testing week.

STEP 8: INDIVIDUALIZE THE PROGRAMME

When planning the previous step, allow for the facilities available to you, using the suggested alternatives where necessary. It is important to appreciate that no alternative exercises can be used for maximum strength training for safety issues.

STEP 9: INSERT TESTING DATES

Ideally the test dates should be scheduled to coincide with recovery weeks. Take the battery of tests at the point where the training programme begins; test days are then scheduled for the beginning and end of the off-season. Testing should also be performed twice during the in-season at regular spaced intervals that coincide with recovery weeks. The initial training year may see some irregularities in the spacing of the test dates. The following years allow the testing to be performed at regular intervals (*see* Table 55).

STEP 10: STARTING THE PROGRAMME

The design of the training programme is such that the largest gains in fitness occur as a result of the gradual increase in intensity over the duration of the off-season. Fitness levels can still be increased during the in-season, especially when beginning the training programme. The key to improving fitness levels during the in-season is the scheduling of both development and recovery blocks to allow time to be focused upon improving your fitness levels and recovery.

SUMMARY

By applying these ten steps with the use of the reference tables and blank forms in the Appendix, you can prepare your own twelve-month conditioning programme. The example programme in the next chapter will show you how this yearly planning is co-ordinated.

CHAPTER 8
A Sample Training Programme

This chapter gives a year-long example of a conditioning programme. The player began his training in March, and the following twelve months of training have been presented here. By looking at how the year-long programme was performed, the way to structure your own training programme should become clear and therefore implemented into your life.

When reviewing this chapter try to take note of how he inserted extra development weeks into the in-season to increase his fitness and how he made allowances for the lack of facilities, time and injury during the training year. The test data tables shows a lot of information about the athlete. You can see how this aids as a motivational tool as you strive to better previous performances. The training block planners shows how the progressions are applied within a protocol and should clarify when to use each training method.

TEST DATA

Name: James Cheeseman.

Position: Winger.

Exercise/Date	14 March	1 May	29 Aug	4 Nov	Notes
TABLE 56: TEST RESULTS DATA TABLE					
Body composition					
Weight (kg)	71	74	70	72	
Body fat (%)	19.5	18.5	13	12	
Flexibility					
Overhead squat	Fail	Fail	Pass	Pass	
Hip flexor test	Fail	Fail	Pass	Pass	
Back twist	Fail	Pass	Pass	Pass	
Reverse press up	Fail	Pass	Pass	Pass	
Knees to chest	Pass	Pass	Pass	Pass	
Power & agility					
Vertical jump (cm)	50cm	50cm	59cm	59cm	
T-Test (sec)	10.8 sec	N/A	9.9 sec	9.9 sec	
3 rep max –					
Deadlift	65 kg	77.5kg	110kg	112.5kg	
Squat	70kg	80kg	107.5kg	107.5kg	
Bent over row	50kg	60kg	85kg	90kg	
Bench press	55kg	60kg	82.5kg	80kg	
Sprints (sec)					
40m	6.8	N/A	5.5	5.6*	
100m	13.6	N/A	12.1	12.3*	
400m	65	63	56	55*	
Aerobic test					
6min run	1300m	1400m	1910m	1750m*	*waterlogged pitch
Other:					
Weather conditions	Dry and calm	Dry and calm	Dry and calm	Rainy and blustery	
Pitch conditions	Firm	Firm	Firm	Soggy	
Notes				The wet pitch altered my results	

TABLE 57: THE YEARLY PLANNER OVERVIEW 8 MARCH TO 30 AUGUST

Week	Mar 8–29	Apr 5	Apr 12	Apr 19–26	May 3–24	May 31–Jun 14	Jun 21	Jun 28–Jul 26	Aug 2–16	Aug 23	Aug 30
Season	In-season	In-season	In-season	Off-season	Off-season	In-Season	In-Season	In-Season	In-Season	In-Season	In-season
Block	Maintenance	Dev	Maint	Rec	Basic fitness preparation	General fitness preparation	Recovery	Sport-specific preparation	Position-specific preparation	Recovery	Maint
Aerobic endurance training	Maintenance	Spec end	Maint	No formal training	Steady pace	Intervals & recovery	Recovery	Intervals & rest	Special endurance	Recovery	Maint
Sprint training	Maintenance	0–60m	Maint	No formal training	300m	200m	–	100m	0–60m	–	Maint
Plyometric training	Maintenance	High specific	Maint	No formal training	Low intensity	Medium intensity	–	Medium intensity	Medium intensity specific	–	Maint
Strength training	Maintenance	Speed strength	Maint	No formal training	Preparation	General hypertrophy	Recovery	Specific hypertrophy	Speed strength	Recovery	Maint
Agility training	Maintenance	Rugby move	Maint	No formal training	Foundation movements	Basic movements	–	Combination movements	Rugby-specific movements	–	Maint
Core training	Maintenance	Strength	Maint	No formal training	Preparation	Endurance	–	Strength	Strength	–	Maint

TABLE 58: THE YEARLY PLANNER OVERVIEW 6 SEPTEMBER TO 28 FEBRUARY

Week	Sep 6	Sep 13	Sep 20	Sep 27	Oct 4	Oct 11	Oct 18	Oct 25	Nov 1	Nov 8	Nov 15	Nov 22	Nov 29	Dec 6	Dec 13	Dec 20	Dec 27	Jan 3	Jan 10	Jan 17	Jan 24	Jan 31	Feb 7	Feb 14	Feb 21	Feb 28
Season	In-season																									
Block	Maintenance								Recovery	Development			Maintenance			Dev		Recovery	Maintenance			Dev				Maint
Aerobic training	Maintenance								Recovery	Int + rec	Int + rest	Spec end	Maintenance			Int + rest	Spec end	Recovery	Maintenance			SP	Int + rest	Int + rest	Spec end	Maint
Sprint training	Maintenance								–	200m	100m	0–60m	Maintenance			100m	0–60m	–	Maintenance			300m	200m	100m	0–60m	Maint
Plyometric training	Maintenance								–	Medium	High	High specific	Maintenance			High	High specific	–	Maintenance			Low	Medium	High	High specific	Maint
Strength training	Maintenance								Recovery	Gen hyp	Spec hyp	Speed strength	Maintenance			Spec hyp	Speed strength	Recovery	Maintenance			Prep	Gen hyp	Spec hyp	Speed strength	Maint
Agility training	Maintenance								–	Basic move	Comb move	Rugby move	Maintenance			Comb move	Rugby move	–	Maintenance			Found move	Basic move	Comb move	Rugby move	Maint
Core training	Maintenance								Recovery	Prep	End	Strength	Maintenance			End	Strength	Recovery	Maintenance			Prep	End	Strength	Strength	Maint

151

Period: In-season
Block: Development (1 week)
Dates: 8–14 March
Number of weeks: 3

Notes: No game as Six Nations weekend

TABLE 59: WEEKLY PLANNER

Mon	Tues	Wed	Thurs	Fri	Sat	Sun
Session A	Session B Team training	Session C	Session A Team training	Session B	Session C	Off

Training Protocol

Aerobic Endurance Training

Special endurance 100m course × 20m.

Sprint Training

60, 60, 40, 30, 20m × 1; 2min rest.

Agility Training

Rugby-specific movements, 10m and 25m × 2/exercise; 60sec rest.

Plyometric Training

Medium specific, 2 × 8 reps; 90sec rest.

Resistance Training

Jump squat, push and pull, lunge, cable twist, straight-leg deadlift, incline bench press and bent over row.
   3 × 10 reps*/exercise; 3min rest.

Core Training

Strength: Prone-ball hold, side-ball hold, ball bridge, ball twist, 2 × 60sec per exercise.

Attendance summary (Number of Weeks: 1):
   Session A: 2/2
   Session B: 2/2
   Session C: 2/2
   Team practice: 2/2
   Game: 0/0

Notes: A little stiff from the new training.

---

*Weight used is true 14 rep max.

Period: In-season
Block: Maintenance
Dates: 15 March–4 April
Number of weeks: 3

Notes: None

TABLE 60: WEEKLY PLANNER

Mon	Tues	Wed	Thurs	Fri	Sat	Sun
Session B	Session A Team training	Session C	Session B Team training	Off	Game	Off

Training Protocol

Aerobic Endurance Training

Special endurance course 100m × 20.

Sprint Training

1 × 20, 40, 60, 100, 250, 5min rest between sprints.

Agility Training

Combination (5m and 25m) and rugby-specific movements (10m and 25m), 1 rep/exercise; 60sec rest.

Plyometric Training

Medium specific 1 × 8 reps/exercise; 90sec rest.

Resistance Training

Session 1: Squat, push and pull, straight leg deadlift, cable twist.
    4 sets/exercise of 6* reps, 120sec rest between sets.
Session 2: Squat, push and pull, straight-leg deadlift, bent over row, cable twist, incline bench press, crunch, back raises.
    3 sets/exercise of 6, 9 and 12 reps, 180sec rest between sets.

Core Training

Maintenance: Prone-ball hold, side-ball hold, ball bridge, ball twist, 1 × 30sec/exercise and 1 × 120sec per exercise.

Attendance summary (Number of Weeks: 3):
    Session A: 3/3
    Session B: 6/6
    Session C: 3/3
    Team practice: 4/6
    Game: 3/3

Notes: Missed a couple of team sessions as studying, played well in all three games.

*Using 6 rep max for 2 sets and a lighter weight (true 10 rep max) for 2 sets.

Period: In-season
Block: Development (1 week)
Dates: 5–12 April
Number of weeks: 1

Notes: No game as gap in fixture list

TABLE 61: WEEKLY PLANNER

Mon	Tues	Wed	Thurs	Fri	Sat	Sun
Session B	Session A Team training	Session C	Session B Team training	Off	Off	Session C

Training Protocol

Aerobic Endurance Training

Special endurance course 100m × 20m.

Sprint Training

1 × 60, 60, 40, 30, 20m; 2min rest.

Agility Training

Rugby-specific movements, 10m and 25m × 2/exercise; 60sec rest.

Plyometric Training

Medium specific, 2 × 8 reps; 90sec rest.

Resistance Training

Jump squat, push and pull, lunge, cable twist, straight leg deadlift, incline bench press and bent over row, 3 × 10 reps*/exercise; 180sec rest.

Core Training

Strength: Prone-ball hold, side-ball hold, ball bridge, ball twist, 2 × 60sec per exercise.

Attendance summary (Number of Weeks: 1):
Session A: 2/2
Session B: 2/2
Session C: 2/2
Team practice: 2/2
Game: 0/0

Notes: A solid week of training.

---

*Weight used is true 14 rep max.

Period: In-season
Block: Maintenance
Dates: 12–18 April
Number of weeks: 1

Notes: None

TABLE 62: WEEKLY PLANNER

Mon	Tues	Wed	Thurs	Fri	Sat	Sun
Session B	Session A Team training	Session C	Session B Team training	Off	Game	Off

Training Protocol

Aerobic Endurance Training

Special endurance course, 100m × 20.

Sprint Training

1 × 20, 40, 60, 100, 250, 5min rest between sprints.

Agility Training

Combination (5m and 25m) and rugby-specific movements (10m and 25m), 1 rep/exercise; 60sec rest.

Plyometric Training

Medium-specific 1 × 8 reps/exercise; 90sec rest.

Resistance Training

Session 1: Squat, push and pull, straight-leg deadlift, cable twist.
  4 sets/exercise of 6* reps; 120sec rest.
Session 2: Squat, push and pull, straight-leg deadlift, bent over row, cable twist, incline bench press, crunch, back raises.
  3 sets/exercise of 6, 9 and 12 reps; 180sec rest between sets.

Core Training

Maintenance: Prone-ball hold, side-ball hold, ball bridge, ball twist, 1 × 30sec/exercise and 1 × 120sec per exercise.

Attendance summary (Number of Weeks: 1):
  Session A: 1/1
  Session B: 2/2
  Session C: 1/1
  Team practice: 1/2
  Game: 1/1

Notes: Missed team practice, as had other commitments. Played average, but scored a hat-trick, a good end to the season.

*Using 6 rep max for 2 sets and a lighter weight (true 10 rep max) for 2 sets.

Period: *Off-season*
Block: *Recovery*
Dates: *19 April–1 May*
Number of weeks: *2*

Notes: *Unstructured recovery*

TABLE 63: WEEKLY PLANNER

Mon	Tues	Wed	Thurs	Fri	Sat	Sun
[No formal training]						

Training Protocol

Aerobic Endurance Training

No formal training programme.

Plyometric Training

No formal training programme.

Sprint Training

No formal training programme.

Resistance Training

No formal training programme.

Agility Training

No formal training programme.

Core Training

No formal training programme.

Attendance summary (Number of Weeks: *2*):
   Session A: *0/0*
   Session B: *0/0*
   Session C: *0/0*
   Team practice: *0/0*
   Game: *0/0*

Notes: *Played football with mates a couple of times, good to have some rest, took test data (01/05).*

Period: Off-season
Block: Base fitness preparation
Dates: 3-30 May
Number of weeks: 4

Notes: None

TABLE 64: WEEKLY PLANNER

Mon	Tues	Wed	Thurs	Fri	Sat	Sun
Session A	Session B	Session C	Off	Session A	Session B	Session C

Training Protocol

Aerobic Endurance Training

Steady pace run:
Week 1:	20min
Week 2:	25min
Weeks 3 & 4:	30min

Sprint Training

4 × 300m with rest between sprints of:
Week 1:	3min
Week 2:	6min
Weeks 3 & 4:	9min

Agility Training

Foundation movement exercises:
Week 1:	10m
Week 2:	15m
Weeks 3 & 4:	20m

Plyometric Training

Low intensity exercises, 2 sets/exercise of:
Week 1:	8 reps
Week 2:	10 reps
Weeks 3 & 4:	12 reps

Resistance Training

Preparation protocol: Squat, incline bench press, straight-leg deadlift, bent over row, lunge, shoulder press, push and pull, cable twist, back raises, crunch.
2 sets/exercise, 2min rest between sets of:
Week 1:	15 reps*
Week 2:	10 reps*
Weeks 3 & 4:	5 reps*

Core Training

Preparation: Prone-ball hold, side-ball hold, ball bridge, ball twist.
Week 1:	2 × 30sec per exercise
Week 2:	2 × 60sec per exercise
Weeks 3 & 4:	2 × 90sec per exercise

Attendance summary (Number of Weeks: 4):
    Session A: 8/8
    Session B: 7/8
    Session C: 8/8
    Team practice: 0/0
    Game: 0/0

Notes: Missed a weights session as gym was closed on the Bank Holiday.
Performed one-armed bent over row with a dumb-bell instead of the bent over row exercise, because bar was busy all session.

---

*Not going to failure on last rep, as using lighter weight than maximal.

Period: *Off-season*   Notes: None
Block: *General fitness preparation*
Dates: *31 May–27 June*
Number of weeks: *4*

TABLE 65: WEEKLY PLANNER

Mon	Tues	Wed	Thurs	Fri	Sat	Sun
Session A *Session B*	*Session B*	*Off*	*Session A*	*Session B*	*Session C*	*Off*

Training Protocol

Aerobic Endurance Training

Intervals with recovery, 25min lap running of:
- *Week 1:* *3min: 1min × 5*
- *Week 2:* *2min: 1min × 7*
- *Weeks 3 & 4: 1min: 1min × 10*

Sprint Training:

200m × 4, with rest between reps of:
- *Week 1:* *3min*
- *Week 2:* *6min*
- *Weeks 3 & 4: 9min*

Agility Training

Basic movement drills, 2 sets/exercise; 90sec rest:
- *Week 1:* *20m/exercise*
- *Week 2:* *25m/exercise*
- *Weeks 3 & 4: 30m/exercise*

Attendance summary (Number of weeks: *4*):
- Session A: *8/8*
- Session B: *8/8*
- Session C: *8/8*
- Team Practise: *0/0*
- Game: *0/0*

Plyometric Training

Medium intensity exercises, 2 sets; 90sec rest for:
- *Week 1:* *8 reps*
- *Week 2:* *10 reps*
- *Weeks 3 & 4: 12 reps*

Resistance Training

General hypertrophy, 2 sets/exercise of: Squat, straight-leg deadlift, lunge, bent over row, chin-ups, back-raises, push and pull, incline bench press, shoulder press, cable twists:
- *Week 1:* *12 reps + 30sec rest*
- *Week 2:* *9 reps + 60sec rest*
- *Weeks 3 & 4: 6 reps + 90sec rest*

Core Training

Endurance: Prone-ball hold, side-ball hold, ball bridge, ball twist.
- *Week 1:* *1 × 120sec per exercise*
- *Week 2:* *1 × 135sec per exercise*
- *Weeks 3 & 4: 1 × 150sec per exercise*

Notes: *Performed one-armed bent over row with a dumb-bell instead of the bent over row exercise because bar was again busy all session.*

Period: Off-season
Block: Recovery (structured)
Dates: 28 June–4 July
Number of weeks: 1

Notes: Planned recovery week as half-way through off-season

TABLE 66: WEEKLY PLANNER

Mon	Tues	Wed	Thurs	Fri	Sat	Sun
Off	Session A	Session B	Session C	Off	Off	Off

Training Protocol

Aerobic Endurance Training

15min steady pace run; perform at an easy, comfortable pace.

Sprint Training

10 × 100m; 30sec rest, easy paced.

Agility Training

No agility exercise programme.

Plyometric Training:

No plyometric exercise programme.

Resistance Training

Recovery: Squat, push and pull, lunge, cable twist, back raises, crunch.
  2 sets of 15 reps, 60sec rest, not to failure (use weight of true repetition maximum 20–25 reps).

Core Training

Recovery: Prone-ball hold, side-ball hold, ball bridge, ball twist.
  1 × 30 sec per exercise at low intensity.

Attendance summary (Number of Weeks: 1):
  Session A: 1/1
  Session B: 1/1
  Session C: 1/1
  Team practice: 0/0
  Game: 0/0

Notes: A comfortable week, feel really refreshed and ready to go for the next half of the off-season.

Period: Off-season
Block: Sport-specific preparation
Dates: 5 July–1 August
Number of weeks: 4

Notes: None

TABLE 67: WEEKLY PLANNER

Mon	Tues	Wed	Thurs	Fri	Sat	Sun
Session A	Session B Team training	Session C	Session A Team training	Session B	Session C	Off

Training Protocol

Aerobic Endurance Training

Intervals with rest, lap running of:

Week 1:	6min: 2min × 2
Week 2:	6min: 4min × 2
Weeks 3 & 4:	6min: 6min × 3

Sprint Training

100m × 4, with rest between reps of:

Week 1:	3min rest
Week 2:	6min rest
Weeks 3 & 4:	9min rest

Agility Training

Combination movement drills, 2 sets/exercise; 90sec rest.

Week 1:	5m & 25m/exercise
Week 2:	7.5m & 35m/exercise
Weeks 3 & 4:	10m & 45m/exercise

Plyometric Training

Medium intensity exercises, 90sec rest, 2 sets of:

Week 1:	8 reps
Week 2:	10 reps
Weeks 3 & 4:	12 reps

Resistance Training

Specific hypertrophy straight-leg deadlift, push and pull, squat, incline bench press, bent over row, lunge, cable twist, back raises, crunch:

Week 1:	4 sets of 12 reps, 180sec rest
Week 2:	4 sets of 9 reps, 180sec rest
Weeks 3 & 4:	4 sets of 6 reps, 180sec rest

Core Training

Strength: Prone-ball hold, side-ball hold, ball bridge, ball twist. Strength protocol.

Week 1:	2 × 60sec per exercise
Week 2:	2 × 45sec per exercise
Weeks 3 & 4:	2 × 30sec per exercise

Attendance summary (Number of Weeks: 4):
Session A: 8/8
Session B: 8/8
Session C: 8/8
Team practice: 2/2
Game: 0/0

Notes: Felt really fit going into the team training sessions, huge improvement on last year.

Period: Off-season
Block: Position-specific exercises
Dates: 2–22 August
Number of weeks: 3

Notes: None

TABLE 68: WEEKLY PLANNER

Mon	Tues	Wed	Thurs	Fri	Sat	Sun
Session A	Session B Team training	Session C	Session A Team training	Session B Session C	Off	Off

---

Training Protocol

Aerobic Endurance Training

Special endurance course 100m:
- Week 1: 90m × 20
- Week 2: 90m × 30
- Week 3: 90m × 40

Sprint Training

1 × 20, 30, 40, 60, 60m with rest between sprints of:
- Week 1: 2min
- Week 2: 4min
- Week 3: 6min

Agility Training

Combination movement drills, 2 sets/exercise, 90sec rest:
- Week 1: 5m & 25m
- Week 2: 7.5m & 35m
- Week 3: 10m & 45m

Attendance summary (Number of Weeks: 3):
- Session A: 6/6
- Session B: 6/6
- Session C: 6/6
- Team practice: 2/2
- Game: 0/0

Plyometric Training

Medium intensity specific exercises, 90sec rest, 2 sets of:
- Week 1: 8 reps
- Week 2: 10 reps
- Week 3: 1 2 reps

Resistance Training:

Speed-strength protocol: Jump squat, push and pull, lunge, cable twist, straight-leg deadlift, incline bench press and bent over row.
3 sets per exercise, 3min rest between sets of:
- Week 1: 10* reps
- Week 2: 7* reps
- Week 3: 4* reps

Core Training

Strength: Prone-ball hold, side-ball hold, ball bridge, ball twist.
- Week 1: 2 × 60sec per exercise
- Week 2: 2 × 45sec per exercise
- Week 3+: 2 × 30sec per exercise

Notes: Did all the training Monday to Friday as had to go away each weekend; missed a pre-season friendly game because of this.

---

*With weight of lighter true rep max, for example, using weights of rep max 14, 11, 8 in each week respectively.

Period: Off-season
Block: Recovery (structured)
Dates: 23–30 August
Number of weeks: 1

Notes: End of off-season recovery week

TABLE 69: WEEKLY PLANNER

Mon	Tues	Wed	Thurs	Fri	Sat	Sun
Session A	Session B Team training	Session C	Team training	Off	Game [measurements]	

Training Protocol

Aerobic Endurance Training

15min steady-pace run; perform at an easy, comfortable pace.

Sprint Training

10 × 100m, 30sec rest, easy paced.

Agility Training

No agility exercise programme.

Plyometric Training

No plyometric exercise programme.

Resistance Training

Recovery: Squat, push and pull, lunge, cable twist, back raises, crunch.

2 sets of 15 reps, 60sec rest, not to failure (use weight of true repetition, maximum 20–25 reps).

Core training

Recovery: Prone-ball hold, side-ball hold, ball bridge, ball twist.

1 × 30sec per exercise at low intensity.

Attendance summary (Number of Weeks: 1):
  Session A: 1/1
  Session B: 1/1
  Session C: 1/1
  Team practice: 2/2
  Game: 1/1

Notes: Played only twenty minutes of the game, felt sharp, took measurements, amazing improvements.

Period: In-season
Block: Maintenance
Dates: 31 August–30 October
Number of weeks: 9

Notes: None

TABLE 70: WEEKLY PLANNER

Mon	Tues	Wed	Thurs	Fri	Sat	Sun
Session B	Session A Team training	Session B	Session C Team training	Off	Game	Off

Training Protocol

Aerobic Endurance Training

Special endurance course 100m × 20.

Sprint Training

1 × 20, 40, 60, 100, 250, 5min rest between sprints.

Agility Training

Combination (5m & 25m) and rugby-specific movements (10m & 25m), 1 rep/exercise; 1min rest.

Plyometric Training

Medium specific 1 × 8 reps/exercise, 90sec rest.

Resistance Training

Session 1: Squat, push and pull, straight leg deadlift, cable twist.
   4 sets/exercise of 6* reps, 120sec rest.
Session 2: Squat, push and pull, straight-leg deadlift, bent over row, cable twist, incline bench press, crunch, back raises.
   3 sets/exercise of 6, 9 and 12 reps, 180sec rest between sets.

Core Training

Maintenance: Prone-ball hold, side-ball hold, ball bridge, ball twist, 1 × 30sec/exercise and 1 × 120sec per exercise.

Attendance summary (Number of Weeks: 9):
   Session A: 9/9
   Session B: 14/18
   Session C: 8/9
   Team practice: 15/18
   Game: 9/9

Notes: A few sessions missed through injuries picked up in games. I have been playing fantastically well, top try scorer and feeling quick, strong and fit.

---

*Using 6 rep max for 2 sets and a lighter weight (true 10 rep max) for 2 sets.

Period: In-season
Block: Recovery (structured)
Dates: 1–7 November
Number of weeks: 1

Note: Planned to allow the body to recover from previous nine games

---

TABLE 71: WEEKLY PLANNER

Mon	Tues	Wed	Thurs	Fri	Sat	Sun
Session A	Session B Team training	Session C	Measure-ments	Off	Game	Off

Training Protocol

Aerobic Endurance Training

15min steady-pace run, performed at an easy, comfortable pace.

Sprint Training

10 × 100m, 30sec rest, easy paced.

Agility Training

No agility exercise programme.

Plyometric Training

No plyometric exercise programme.

Resistance Training

Recovery: Squat, push and pull, lunge, cable twist, back raises, crunch.

2 sets of 15 reps, 60sec rest, not to failure (use weight of true repetition maximum 20–25 reps).

Core Training

Recovery: Prone-ball hold, side-ball hold, ball bridge, ball twist.

1 × 30sec per exercise at low intensity.

Attendance summary (Number of Weeks: 1):
    Session A: 1/1
    Session B 1/1
    Session C: 1/1
    Team practice: 2/2
    Game: 1/1

Notes: Took test data, more improvements, very happy.

Period: In-season
Block: Development (3 weeks)
Dates: 8–28 November
Number of weeks: 3

Notes: No game due to November internationals

TABLE 72: WEEKLY PLANNER

Mon	Tues	Wed	Thurs	Fri	Sat	Sun
Session A	Session B Team training	Off	Session C Team training	Off	Session A	Session B Session C

Training Protocol

Aerobic Endurance Training

Week 1: 3min: 1min recovery × 5
Week 2: 6min: 2min rest × 2
Week 3: Special endurance course 100m × 20

Sprint Training

Week 1: 200m × 4, 3min rest
Week 2: 100m × 4, 3min rest
Week 3: 20m, 30m, 40m, 60m, 60m × 1, 2min rest

Agility Training

Basic, combination and rugby-specific movements protocols:
Week 1: Basic movement drills, 20m, 2 sets/exercise, 90sec rest
Week 2: Combination movements 5m & 25m, 2 sets/exercise, 90sec rest
Week 3: Rugby-specific movements: 10m & 25m, 2 sets/exercise, 90sec rest

Plyometric Training

Week 1: Medium intensity drills, 2 × 8 reps/exercise, 90sec rest
Week 2: High intensity drills, 2 × 8 reps/exercise, 90sec rest
Week 3: High specific intensity drills, 2 × 8 reps/exercise, 90sec rest

Resistance Training

Week 1: General hypertrophy exercises 2 × 12 reps/exercise, 30sec rest
Week 2: Specific hypertrophy exercises 3 × 12 reps/exercise, 180sec rest
Week 3: Speed strength exercises 3 × 10* reps/exercise, 180sec rest

Core Training

Preparation, endurance and strength protocol.
Week 1: 2 × 30sec exercise
Week 2: 1 × 120sec exercise
Week 3: 2 × 60sec exercise

Attendance summary (Number of Weeks: 3):
Session A: 6/6
Session B: 6/6
Session C: 6/6
Team practice: 6/6
Game: 0/0

Notes: Using high intensity exercises for plyometrics as last test day showed, I now have sufficient leg strength to fulfil the criteria.

*Using weight of true 14 rep max.

Period: In-season
Block: Maintenance
Dates: 29 November–19 December
Number of weeks: 3

Notes: None

TABLE 73: WEEKLY PLANNER

Mon	Tues	Wed	Thurs	Fri	Sat	Sun
Session B	Session A Team training	Session C	Session B Team training	Off	Game	Off

Training Protocol

Aerobic Endurance Training

Special endurance course 100m × 20.

Sprint Training

1 × 20, 40, 60, 100, 250, 5min rest between sprints.

Agility Training

Combination (5m and 25m) and rugby-specific movements (10m and 25m), 1 rep/exercise. 1min rest.

Plyometric Training

High intensity specific exercises, 1 × 8 reps/exercise, 90sec rest.

Resistance Training

session 1: Squat, push and pull, straight leg deadlift, cable twist.
  4 sets/exercise of 6* reps, 120sec rest.
session 2: Squat, push and pull, straight-leg deadlift, bent over row, cable twist, incline bench press, crunch, back raises.
  3 sets/exercise of 6, 9 and 12 reps, 180sec rest between sets.

Core Training

Maintenance: Prone-ball hold, side-ball hold, ball bridge, ball twist.
  1 × 30sec/exercise and 1 × 120sec per exercise.

Attendance summary (Number of Weeks: 3):
  Session A: 3/3
  Session B: 6/6
  Session C: 3/3
  Team practice: 6/6
  Game: 3/3

Notes: Still playing well, top try scorer, feel good and confident in games. Coach commended my attendance and said I am a vastly improved player.

*Using 6 rep max for 2 sets and a lighter weight (true 10 rep max) for 2 sets.

Period: *In-season*
Block: *Development (2 week)*
Date: *20 December–2 January*
Number of weeks: *2*

Note: *No game or team practices due to Christmas*

TABLE 74: WEEKLY PLANNER

Mon	Tues	Wed	Thurs	Fri	Sat	Sun
Session A	Session B Session C	Off	Off	Session A	Session B Session C	Off

Training Protocol

Aerobic Endurance Training

Intervals with rest and special endurance:
- Week 1: 6min work: 2min rest × 2 work intervals
- Week 2: Special endurance course 100m × 20

Sprint Training

200m, 100m and 0–60m:
- Week 1: 100m × 4, 3min rest between reps
- Week 2: 20m, 30m, 40m, 60m, 60m × 1, 2min rest

Agility Training

Combination and rugby-specific movements:
- Week 1: Combination movements 5m and 25m, 2 sets/exercise, 90sec rest
- Week 2: Rugby-specific movements: 10m and 25m, 2 sets/exercise/ 90sec rest

Plyometric Training

High and high specific exercises:
- Week 1: High intensity drills, 2 × 8 reps/exercise, 90sec rest
- Week 2: High specific intensity drills, 2 × 8 reps/exercise, 90sec rest

Resistance Training

Specific hypertrophy and speed strength:
- Week 1: Specific hypertrophy exercises 3 × 12 reps/exercise, 180sec rest
- Week 2: Speed strength exercises 3 × 10* reps/exercise, 180sec rest

Core Training

Endurance and strength protocols.
- Week 1: 1 × 120sec per exercise
- Week 2: 2 × 60sec per exercise

Attendance summary (Number of Weeks: 2):
Session A: *4/4*
Session B: *2/4*
Session C: *4/4*
Team practice: *0/0*
Game: *0/0*

Notes: *Missed a couple of resistance-training sessions as gym was closed over Christmas. Really enjoying the high intensity plyometrics.*

*Using weight of true 14 rep max.

Period: *In-season*
Block: *Recovery (structured)*
Dates: *2–8 January*
Number of weeks: *1*

Notes: *Planned to allow the body to recover from previous games and training*

TABLE 75: WEEKLY PLANNER

Mon	*Tues*	*Wed*	*Thurs*	*Fri*	*Sat*	*Sun*
Session A	Session B Team training	Session C	Team training	Off	Game	Off

Training Protocol

Aerobic Endurance Training

15min steady pace run, perform at easy comfortable pace.

Sprint Training

10 × 100m, 30sec rest, easy paced.

Agility Training

No agility exercise programme.

Plyometric Training

No plyometric exercise programme.

Resistance Training

Recovery: Squat, push and pull, lunge, cable twist, back raises, crunch.

2 sets of 15 reps, 60sec rest, not to failure (use weight of true repetition maximum 20–25 reps).

Core Training

Recovery: Prone-ball hold, side-ball hold, ball bridge, ball twist.

1 × 30sec per exercise at low intensity.

Attendance summary (Number of Weeks: 1):
Session A: *1/1*
Session B: *1/1*
Session C: *1/1*
Team practice: *1/2*
Game: *1/1*

Notes: *Asked to be excused from team session to aid recovery.*

Period: *In-season*
Block: *Maintenance*
Dates: *10 January–7 February*
Number of weeks: *4*

Notes: *None*

TABLE 76: WEEKLY PLANNER

Mon	Tues	Wed	Thurs	Fri	Sat	Sun
Session B	Session A Team training	Session C	Session B Team training	Off	Game	Off

---

Training Protocol

Aerobic Endurance Training

Special endurance course 100m × 20.

Sprint Training

1 × 20, 40, 60, 100, 250, 5min rest between sprints.

Agility Training

Combination (5m and 25m) and rugby-specific movements (10m and 25m), rep/exercise; 1min rest.

Plyometric Training

High intensity specific 1 × 8 reps/exercise; 90sec rest.

Resistance Training

session 1: Squat, push and pull, straight-leg deadlift, cable twist.
   4 sets/exercise of 6* reps; 120sec rest.
session 2: Squat, push & pull, straight-leg deadlift, bent over row, cable twist, incline bench press, crunch, back raises.
   3 sets/exercise of 6, 9 and 12 reps, 180sec rest between sets.

Core Training

Maintenance: Prone-ball hold, side-ball hold, ball bridge, ball twist, 1 × 30sec/exercise and 1 × 120sec per exercise.

Attendance summary (Number of Weeks: 3):
   Session A: 4/4
   Session B: 8/8
   Session C: 4/4
   Team practice: 8/8
   Games: 4/4

Notes: *Slight injuries meant I couldn't perform all the weight-training exercises during some sessions.*

---

*Using 6 rep max for 2 sets and a lighter weight (true 10 rep max) for 2 sets.

Period: In-season
Block: Development (3 weeks)
Dates: 7–27 February
Number of weeks: 3

Notes: Decided to place a development block despite the friendly fixture

TABLE 77: WEEKLY PLANNER

Mon	Tues	Wed	Thurs	Fri	Sat	Sun
Session A Session B	Session C Team training	Session B	Session A Team training	Session C	Game	Off

Training Protocol

Aerobic Endurance Training

Week 1: 3min; 1min recovery × 5
Week 2: 6 min; 2min rest × 2
Week 3: Special endurance course 100m × 20

Sprint Training

Week 1: 200m × 4, 3min rest
Week 2: 100m × 4, 3min rest
Week 3: 20m, 30m, 40m, 60m, 60m × 1, 2min rest

Agility Training

Basic, combination and rugby-specific movements:

Week 1: Basic movement drills, 20m/2 sets/exercise, 90sec rest
Week 2: Combination movements 5m and 25m, 2 sets/exercise, 90sec rest
Week 3: Rugby-specific movements: 10m and 25m, 2 sets/exercise/ 90sec rest

Plyometric Training

Week 1: Medium intensity drills, 2 × 8 reps/exercise, 90sec rest
Week 2: High intensity drills, 2 × 8 reps/exercise, 90sec rest
Week 3: High specific intensity drills, 2 × 8 reps/exercise, 90sec rest

Resistance Training

Week 1: General hypertrophy exercises 2 × 12 reps/exercise, 30sec rest
Week 2: Specific hypertrophy exercises 3 × 12 reps/exercise, 180sec rest
Week 3: Speed strength exercises 3 × 10* reps/exercise, 180sec rest

Core Training

Preparation, endurance, and strength protocols.
Week 1: 2 × 30sec per exercise
Week 2: 1 × 120sec per exercise
Week 3: 2 × 60sec per exercise

Attendance summary (Number of Weeks: 3):
Session A: 6/6
Session B: 6/6
Session C: 6/6
Team practice: 6/6
Game: 1/1

Notes: The training scheduled didn't impede performance too much, though I did feel a little more tired than usual.

*Using weight of true 14 rep max.

Period: In-season
Block: Maintenance
Dates: 28 February – 6 March
Number of weeks: 1

Notes: None

TABLE 78: WEEKLY PLANNER

Mon	Tues	Wed	Thurs	Fri	Sat	Sun
Session B	Session A Team training	Session B	Session B Team training	Off	Game	Off

Training Protocol

Aerobic Endurance Training

Special endurance course, 100m × 20.

Sprint Training

1 × 20, 40, 60, 100, 250, 5min rest between sprints.

Agility Training

Combination (5m and 25m) and rugby-specific movements (10m and 25m), 1 rep/exercise. 1min rest.

Plyometric Training

High intensity specific 1 × 8 reps/exercise, 90sec rest.

Resistance Training

session 1: Squat, push and pull, straight-leg deadlift, cable twist.
4 sets/exercise of 6* reps, 120sec rest.

session 2: Squat, push and pull, straight-leg deadlift, bent over row, cable twist, incline bench press, crunch, back raises.
3 sets/exercise of 6, 9 and 12 reps, 180sec rest between sets.

Core Training

Maintenance: Prone-ball hold, side-ball hold, ball bridge, ball twist.
1 × 30sec/exercise and 1 × 120sec per exercise.

Attendance summary (Number of Weeks: 1):
  Session A: 1/1
  Session B: 2/2
  Session C: 1/1
  Team practice: 2/2
  Games: 1/1

Notes: Good to be playing regularly again.

---

*Using 6 rep max for 2 sets and a lighter weight (true 10 rep max) for 2 sets.

Summary

The programme shows how all the training theory and exercises can be brought together to form a powerful and effective conditioning programme that will result in greatly improved levels of fitness and on-field performance.

You should now plan your own programme using the ten steps set out in Chapter 7 and the charts in the Appendix. This will allow you to create a provisional year-long conditioning programme. Once completed, alterations can be made as needed during the year, depending on fixture changes, team selection, injuries and suchlike.

Appendix

Follow steps 1–10 in Chapter 7 and use the blank tables to plan out your training schedule for the coming twelve months. The whole year can be set out immediately, but should be done in pencil to allow for changes in circumstances.

Use the reference charts as an aid in designing the block structure, and to transfer the training protocols into the programme when designing your conditioning programme (*see* Tables 79 and 80).

The appendix contains the forms and all the information you will need to create your own twelve month conditioning routine. To do this, review the ten steps in chapter seven and then sequentially apply them using the resources here. Use the yearly planner forms to provisionally draw up the structure for the year ahead. Remember to do this in pencil as the changes to fixture list, the team and injury can all alter your training requirements.

With the training blocks for the year planned out use the relevant data tables to draw up the training you will be performing within each training method. This will allow you to know exactly what training you will be performing for the whole of the next year subject to changes from other outside influences.

During the training year review your training plan daily to know exactly what sessions you should be doing. Use chapter three to give you the details of how to perform each exercise. Make alterations as and when to the program under your discretion, e.g. inserting a recovery week if feel drained, etc.

Finally, it is always a good idea to review the science and reasons behind why you are doing the training and what is necessary to receive optimum benefits from it. The theory of training is covered in chapter one, two and five.

As a conditioning specialist and an enthusiastic coach I wish you every success in your rugby career and hope you achieve all your goals within the game. If you to wish to learn more about conditioning please feel free to browse the website www.rugbyfitnesstraining.com. This site contains further information pertinent to your on-field performance, including nutrition and latest research. If you experiencing any problems you can contact me on info@rugbyfitnesstraining.co.uk.

Ben Wilson

TABLE 79: THE YEARLY PLANNER

Week																		
Season																		
Block																		
Aerobic endurance training																		
Sprint training																		
Plyometric training																		
Strength training																		
Agility training																		
Core training																		

TABLE 80: THE YEARLY PLANNER

Week									
Season									
Block									
Aerobic endurance training									
Sprint training									
Plyometric training									
Strength training									
Agility training									
Core training									

TRAINING BLOCK PLANNER

Period: Notes:
Block:
Dates:
Number of weeks:

Mon	Tues	Wed	Thurs	Fri	Sat	Sun

Training Protocol

Aerobic Endurance Training   *Plyometric Training*

Sprint Training   *Resistance Training*

Agility Training   *Core Training*

Attendance summary (Number of weeks: _)
   Session A: /   Notes:
   Session B: /
   Session C: /
   Team practice: /
   Game: /

TEST DATA

Name:

Age:

Position:

TABLE 82: TEST RESULTS DATA TABLE

Exercise/date					Notes
Body composition					
Weight (KG)					
Body fat (%)					
Flexibility					
Overhead squat					
Thomas's test					
Back twist					
Reverse press up					
Knees to chest					
Power & agility					
Vertical jump (cm)					
T-Test (sec)					
3 Rep max –					
Deadlift					
Squat					
Bent over row					
Bench press					
Sprints (sec)					
40m					
100m					
400m					
Aerobic test					
6min run					
Other:					
Weather conditions					
Pitch conditions					
Notes					

BLOCK STRUCTURE FOR A SHORTENED OFF-SEASON

TABLE 83: BLOCK STRUCTURE FOR A SHORTEREN OFF-SEASON OF LESS THAN FIFTEEN WEEKS IN LENGH

Length of off-season	May			June				July				August		
	17	24	31	7	14	21	28	5	12	19	26	2	9	16	23
15 weeks	R	B		Gen				R	SS			PS			R
14 weeks	–	R	B		Gen				R	SS			PS		R
13 weeks	–	–	R	B		Gen				R	SS			PS	R
12 weeks	–	–	–	R	B		Gen			R	SS			PS	R
11 weeks	–	–	–	–	R	B		Gen		R	SS			PS	R
10 weeks	–	–	–	–	–	R	B		Gen		SS			PS	R
9 weeks	–	–	–	–	–	–	R	B		Gen				SS	R
8 weeks	–	–	–	–	–	–	–	R	B		Gen			SS	R
7 weeks	–	–	–	–	–	–	–	–	R	B		Gen			R
6 weeks	–	–	–	–	–	–	–	–	–	B			Gen		R
5 weeks	–	–	–	–	–	–	–	–	–	–	B			Gen	R
4 weeks	–	–	–	–	–	–	–	–	–	–	–	B			R
3 weeks	–	–	–	–	–	–	–	–	–	–	–	–	B	B	R
2 weeks	–	–	–	–	–	–	–	–	–	–	–	–	–	B	R
1 week	–	–	–	–	–	–	–	–	–	–	–	–	–	–	R

Key: B – Base fitness preparation, Gen – General fitness preparation, SS – Sport-specific training, PS – Position-specific preparation.

TRAINING PROTOCOL SUMMARIES

The following tables state all the training protocol that can be used in the six training methods throughout the course of the year (*see* Tables 84–92).

TABLE 84: SUMMARY OF AEROBIC ENDURANCE TRAINING

Protocol	Running type	Progression (reps)		
		Week 1	Week 2	Week 3+
Steady pace	Lap or straight line	20min	25min	30min
Intervals & recovery	Traditional, lap or line.	3min : 1min × 5	2min : 1min × 7	1min : 1min × 10
Intervals & rest	Traditional, lap or line.	6min : 2min × 3	6min : 1min × 3	6min : 6min × 3
Special endurance	Line running – 80/90m special endurance course	20 reps	30 reps	40 reps
Maintenance	Line running	20 reps × Special endurance 80/100m course.		
Recovery	Traditional or lap.	15min comfortable steady pace run.		

Key: 1 min : 1 min × 10 – 1min at higher work level, 1min recovery (slower speed) or rest, × 10 – Perform 10 repetitions of the work period.

TABLE 85: SUMMARY OF SPRINT TRAINING

Protocol	Exercise	Reps	Progression (rest)		
			Week 1	Week 2	Week 3+
300m	300m	4	3min	6min	9min
200m	200m	4	3min	6min	9min
100m	100m	4	3min	6min	9min
0–60m	Forwards – 60m, 40m, 30m, 20m 20m, Backs – 60m, 60m, 40m,30m, 20m	1	2min	4min	6min
Maintenance	20m, 40m, 60m, 100m, 250m	1	5min		
Recovery	100m	10	30sec		

TABLE 86: SUMMARY OF AGILITY TRAINING

Protocol	Exercises	Reps/ exercise	Rest	Progression (distance)		
				Week 1	Week 2	Week 3+
Foundation movement	Lateral run, back pedal, forward & backward diagonal running.	2 / exercise/ direction	60sec	10	15	20
Basic movement	Weaving run, forward & backward zigzag running. Turn & run shuttle.	2	60sec	20m	25m	30m
Combination movement	Square drill, diamond drill, forward facing Z-pattern runs, lateral weaving run.	2	60sec	5m & 25m	7.5m & 35m	10m & 45m
Rugby-specific movement	Forward facing Z-pattern run with side step, zigzag run with side step, cross agility drill, sideways facing Z-pattern run.	2	60sec	10m & 25m	15m & 35m	20m & 45m
Maintenance	Forward facing Z-pattern run with side step, zigzag run with side step, cross agility drill, sideways facing Z-pattern run, Sqaure drill, diamond drill.	1	60sec	10m & 25m for rugby specific movements. 5m & 25m combination movement exercises.		

TABLE 87: SUMMARY OF PLYOMETRIC TRAINING

Protocol	Exercises	Reps/ exercise	Rest	Progression (reps)		
				Week 1	Week 2	Week 3+
Low intensity	Squat jumps, standing long jump, diagonal jumps, lateral jumps.	2	90sec	8	10	12
Medium intensity	Split-squat jump, double-leg hop, double-leg zigzag hop, sideways jumping.	2	90sec	8	10	12
Medium intensity specific	Cycled split-squat with movement, double-leg hop + 15m lateral run, double leg hop & 15m forward sprint, lateral cone hop & 15m turn and sprint.	2	90sec	8	10	12
High intensity	Single-leg squat jump, single-arm bound, single-leg zigzag hop, single-leg lateral hop.	2	90sec	8 & 20m	10 & 25m	12 & 30m
High intensity specific	Single-leg hop & 15m lateral run, double arm bound, single leg hop & 15m sprint, single-leg lateral hop with 15m turn & sprint.	2	90sec	8 & 20m	10 & 25m	12 & 30m
Maintenance	Medium or high intensity specific exercises.	1	90sec	8 & 20m		

TABLE 88: SUMMARY OF RESISTANCE TRAINING

Protocol	Exercises	Technique	Sets	Progression (reps + rest)		
				Week 1	Week 2	Week 3+
Preparation	Squat, incline bench press, straight-leg deadlift, bent over row, lunge, shoulder press, push & pull, cable twist, back raises, crunch.	Alternative (not to failure)	2	15 & 120sec	10 & 120sec	5 & 120sec
General Hypertrophy	Squat, straight-leg deadlift, lunge, bent over row, chin ups, back raises, push and pull, incline bench press, shoulder press, cable twists, crunch	Consecutive	2	12 & 30sec	9 & 60sec	6 & 90sec
Specific hypertrophy	Straight-leg deadlift, push & pull, squat, incline bench press, bent over row, lunge, cable twist, back raises, crunch.	Alternative – explosive	3	12 & 180sec	9 & 180sec	6 & 180sec
Speed strength	Jump squat, push and pull, lunge, cable twist, straight leg deadlift, incline bench press and bent over row.	Alternative – explosive	3	10 & 180sec	7 & 180sec	4 & 180sec
Slow-speed strength	Squat, incline bench press, straight leg deadlift, bent over row	Alternative – explosive	4	6 & 180sec	4 & 180sec	2 & 180 sec
Maintenance	1. Squat, push & pull, straight leg deadlift, cable twist	Alternative – explosive	4	6* & 180sec		
	2. Squat, push & pull, straight leg deadlift, bent over row, cable twist, incline bench press, crunch, back raises		3	6, 9 , 12 & 180sec		
Recovery	Squat, push & pull, lunge, cable twist, back raises, crunch	Alternative – not to failure	2	15 & 120sec		

*Using 6 rep max for 2 sets and a lighter weight (true 10 rep max) for 2 sets.

TABLE 89: SUMMARY OF CORE TRAINING

Protocol	Exercises	Technique	Sets	Progression (reps + rest)		
				Week 1	Week 2	Week 3+
Preparation	Prone ball hold, side ball hold, ball bridge, ball twist.	Circuit training	2	30sec	60sec	90sec
Endurance	Prone ball hold, side ball hold, ball bridge, ball twist.	Circuit training	1	120sec	135sec	150sec
Strength	Prone ball hold, side ball hold, ball bridge, ball twist.	Circuit training	2	60sec	45sec	30sec
Maintenence	Prone ball hold, side ball hold, ball bridge, ball twist.	Circuit training	2	Ball position and weight used		
Recovery	Prone ball hold, side ball hold, ball bridge, ball twist.	Circuit training	1	None		

TABLE 90: RANKING OF RESISTANCE EXERCISES ACCORDING TO SPECIFICITY

Target area	Exercises	Order of specificity
Legs	Squat Straight-leg deadlift Jump squats Lunge Step-ups One-legged squats Reverse leg press Smith machine squats Leg press Leg extension Leg curl Calf raises	High ↓ Low
Upper body – Pushing	Bench press incline Push and pull One armed push Bench press Shoulder press Dips Lateral raise Triceps pulldown	High ↓ Low
Upper body – Pulling	Bent over row Chin-ups One-armed pulls Push and pull Low row Seated machine row T-bar row Biceps curls	High ↓ Low
Trunk	Cable twist Back extensions Crunch Medicine ball pass Superman Various abdominal exercises	High ↓ Low

TABLE 91: SUMMARY OF SESSIONS PER WEEK TO BE PERFORMED, AND TRAINING BLOCK

Season	Training block	Number of sessions performed /week		
		Session A	Session B	Session C
	Recovery	0	0	0
	Base fitness training	2	2	2
	General fitness preparation	2	2	2
Off-season	Sport-specific preparation	2	2	2
	Position-specific preparation	2	2	2
	Maintenance	1	2	1
In-season	Development	2	2	2
	Recovery	1	1	1

TABLE 92: STRETCH TESTS AND THEIR SUGGESTED STRETCHES

Stretch test	Stretches to perform if failed test
Overhead squat	Calf stretch, hamstring stretch, hip stretch, reverse press-up and chest stretch
Back twist	Back twist stretch, chest stretch, and hip stretch
Knees to chest	Knees to chest stretch, split leg hamstring stretch
Reverse press-up	Reverse press-up
Hip-flexor test	Hip flexor stretch (on object)
Stretch tightness test	The appropriate stretch that failed during these tests
Stretch comparison test	The side that feels particularly tight

Notes

1. www.irb.com.
2. Tudor O Bompa, 1999, *Periodization: Theory and methodology of training*, (Human Kinetics).
3. www.nsca-lift.org.
4. William D. McArdle, Frank I. Katch, Victor L. Kaych, 1999, *Sports & exercise nutrition*. (Lippincott, Williams & Wilkins).
5. S.L. Plisk MS CSCS D*, M.H. Stone PhD, 2003, 'Periodization strategies', J. Strength & Cond. 25(6) pp. 19–37.
6. Bill Foran, 2001 *High performance sports conditioning*, (Human Kinetics). Chapter 4, p. 64.
7. George Dintinman, Bob Ward, Tom Tellez, 1998, *Sports speed* (Human Kinetics).
8. M.U. Deutsch, G.J. Maw, D. Jenkins, P. Raeburn, 1998, *Heart rate, blood lactate and kinematic data of elite colts (under-19) rugby union players during competition*, (University of Queensland, Australia).
9. Grant M. Duthie, 2000, *Descriptive analysis of sprint patterns in super 12*, (Department of Physiology, Australian Institute of Sport, Canberra).
10. H. Seyle, 1976, 'Forty years of stress research: Principal remaining problems & misconceptions', Can. Med. Assoc. J., 115(1) pp. 53–56.
11. James C. Radcliffe and Robert C. Farentnos, 1999, *High powered plyometrics*, (Human Kinetics).
12. Donald A. Chu, 1998, *Jumping into plyometrics* (Human Kinetics).
13. G. Gregory Haff, PhD, CSCS, 2004, 'Roundtable discussion: Periodization of training – Part 1 & 2', J. Strength Conditioning research. 26(1) pp. 50–69, 26(2) pp. 56–70.
14. Thomas R. Baechle, Roger W. Earle, 2000, *Essential of strength training & conditioning*, (Human Kinetics).
15. M.H. Stone, H. O'Bryant, J. Garhammer, 1981, 'A hypothetical model for strength training', J. Sports Med. Phys. Fit 21(4) pp. 342–351.
16. M.H. Stone, H. O'Bryant, J. Garhammer, 1982, 'A theoretical model for strength training', J. Strength & Cond. 4(4) pp. 36–39.

Index